NATURE, CULTURE, AND BIG OLD TREES

NATURE, CULTURE, AND BIG OLD TREES

Live Oaks and Ceibas in the Landscapes of Louisiana and Guatemala

KIT ANDERSON

University of Texas Press, Austin

Requests for permission to reproduce material from this work should be sent to Permissions, University of Texas Press, P.O. Box 7819, Austin, TX 78713-7819.

∞ The paper used in this book meets the minimum requirements of ANSI/NISO Z39.48-1992 (R1997) (Permanence of Paper).

Library of Congress Cataloging-in-Publication Data

Anderson, Katharine.
    Nature, culture, and big old trees : tales of live oaks and ceibas in the landscapes of Louisiana and Guatemala / Kit Anderson — 1st ed.
        p.   cm.
    ISBN 0-292-70212-4 (cl. : alk. paper) — ISBN 292-70213-2 (pbk. : alk. paper)
    1. Oak—Louisiana—Anecdotes.   2. Kapok—Guatemala—Anecdotes.   3. Tress—Symbolic aspects—Anecdotes.   4. Anderson, Katharine.   I. Title.
QK495.F14 A53   2004
583'.46—DC22
                                                                2003016598

Dedicated to my mother

Elisabeth Hamilton Anderson
(1919–1971)

CONTENTS

MAPS

ACKNOWLEDGMENTS

THE IDEA FOR THIS BOOK germinated in 1992, amid a grove of live oaks in Baton Rouge, Louisiana. Professor Miles Richardson had taken his "Place and Culture" class outdoors. Gesturing around at the huge trees under which we stood, he explained they had been planted as memorials to LSU students killed in World War I. Then he asked, "Why live oaks? Why not pines?" That started my quest to better understand the taken-for-granted landscapes around us, and particularly the role of long-lived trees. During the years that followed, Miles was chief mentor, critic, and friend as I pursued my dissertation research and grappled with questions of nature, culture, and big old trees. He accompanied me on several field trips, cheerfully reviewed truly rough drafts, and was always ready to talk. To him and to all such creative and demanding advisors, I give profound thanks.

The two other members of my dissertation committee at Louisiana State University were also crucial to this study. My great thanks to William V. Davidson, of the Department of Geography and Anthropology, who generously shared his information, photographs, and enthusiasm about ceiba trees and contributed important insights on their role in Central America; and to Neil Odenwald, of the Department of Landscape Architecture, who supplied key information and contacts about the trees he knows and loves so well. Special thanks also to Kent Mathewson, Suzanne Turner, and Richard Condrey.

I am deeply grateful for the financial support that enabled me to complete this study. Louisiana State University gave a generous four-year graduate fellowship for doctoral studies. Fieldwork in Guatemala was made possible by two grants from the Robert C. West Field Research Awards, Department of Geography and Anthropology, and a third from the local chapter of Sigma Xi.

Librarians who know their collections well and assist researchers like myself are among the people I cannot thank enough. Among the collections at which I found invaluable help are LSU's Hill Memorial Library (rich in plantation diaries and maps); Tulane University's Latin America collection; the University of Southwestern Louisiana's library (which has Edwin Stephens' papers from the early days of the Live Oak Society); the St. Martinville, Louisiana, public library; the Centro de Investigaciones Regionales de Mesoamérica, a privately funded collection of Latin American studies in Antigua; and the small town library in Palencia, Guatemala. Verlyn Bercegeay, former secretary of the Live Oak Society, allowed me to search through historical records and answered many questions. The society's list of tree-members is now online (louisianagarden clubs.com).

Among those who gave generously of their time to talk about trees are, in Louisiana, Paul Orr, Randy Harris, Jim Foret Sr., Jim Foret Jr., Betty Baggert, Glenn Conrad, Derek Green, Gercie Daigle, Phil Thompson, and Steele Burden (deceased); in Guatemala, Juana Itzol Faulkner, Alfonso Arrivillaga, Francisco Cane Acosta, Edgar Geovany Mendoza, Helen De Soto, and Mike Shawcross. Many others helped me find specific trees, told me their own tree stories, and even welcomed me into their homes during my travels. My thanks to all of them.

Fieldnotes from the years of "oaking" in Louisiana bear the names of adventurous friends who joined me on those expeditions. Many thanks to Kathleen Kennedy, Esther Shaffer, Katie Algeo, Michael Hawkins, Delphine Douglas, Sherri Arnoni, Andy Maxwell, Ily Fernandez, Tanya Kalischer, and Chris Coggins for the hours of driving, recording, mapping, talking, photographing, and laughing as we hunted oaks.

For editorial help and suggestions that vastly improved the final product, many thanks to Cindy Wolcott, Marla Emery, Judy Chaves, Ruth Page, Dan Gade, and Scott Smiley. I also want to thank David

Barrington for giving me office space at the Pringle Herbarium at the University of Vermont while I was writing. Thanks to Shannon Davies (then at UT Press) for her enthusiastic response to the first draft, and to all the current editors there for their meticulous attention to every last detail.

I am especially grateful to David Hoag for preparing the maps for publication and dealing with digital mysteries of production.

Personal thanks for care the feeding of the author go to the Chaves-Heindel family, Dale and Jeanne Goldhaber, the Page family, Regina Hoffman, and many other friends who have borne with me these last eight years.

Thanks to my father for encouragment throughout this process, and for walks among the trees when I was a child. And finally, I'm grateful to my sons, Damon and Toby, for tolerating their tree-crazed mother, staying in touch when I was away from home, helping whenever called upon, and keeping a sense of humor through it all.

NATURE, CULTURE, AND BIG OLD TREES

Chapter 1

INTRODUCTION

HUMAN-TREE RELATIONSHIPS

"Palín, La Ceiba," shouted the bus driver as he pulled over to stop on the highway. I hurried to squeeze through packed bodies to get to the front of the bus, trying not to knock anyone in the head with my backpack, wondering if he had added the bit about ceiba for me, the lone *gringa* in the crowd. It was hot and noisy outside on the highway. A group of us headed up a dusty street that led into town, most with bags and baskets of produce, me with camera, tape measure, notebook, and water bottle. Foreign tourists are rare here. This is a Guatemalan place.

The ceiba is the national tree of Guatemala, and the small town of Palín, about an hour from the capital by bus, has the most famous ceiba in the country. "*Enorma,*" people had said when describing it to me, holding their arms out as if trying to get them around a huge trunk.

Finally I could see something dark ahead, a promise of shade in the glaring hot sunlight of the walled streets. At first it was just a bit of branch reaching into the street, but by the time I reached the church steps, the huge hulking shape of the ceiba had spread out to cover the whole plaza in deep shade. Within the area defined by the generous branches was a bustling market, hundreds of people making their way among piles of brilliantly colored fruits, vegetables, and flowers (Fig. 1.1).

As I stepped into the ceiba's shade, the temperature dropped, the light became comfortably dim, and my eyes focused on the intense activity all around me. Piles of ripe pineapples and tomatoes were

1.1 Palín's famous ceiba tree shelters an entire plaza and bustling market.

arranged next to stalks of izote flowers and cherimoyas; tropical corn, beans, and squash shared blankets with temperate apples and pears. Women weighed produce on hand-held scales, wrapped them in paper or plastic, and handed them over in exchange for coins. Most were *indígenas*, Mayan women identifiable by their distinctive traditional clothing in bright colors. Drawn to the center, where a massive cement structure surrounds the huge, painted trunk of the ceiba, I joined others who sat on the concrete steps. From this raised observation post we could survey the whole market, and the constant activity of bargaining, polishing, sweeping, gossiping, eating, and playing.

Sitting there, sharing my lunch with a vacant-eyed woman who had wordlessly stretched out her hand for food, I was struck by the incredible contrast with another famous tree place I had visited not long ago: Oak Alley in Louisiana. Like Palín, Oak Alley is a well-known place dominated by a symbolic tree species, the Southern live oak. Unlike Palín, Oak Alley is a private place, open to those who have paid an entrance fee. Visitors from all over the world come to tour the gracious antebellum plantation home and to photograph the double row of gnarly old trees that leads from the Mississippi River to a Greek revival mansion (Fig. 1.2). Once an entrance drive connecting house and river, that place today feels more like a sacred grove.

Trees tell stories. In their arrangements, location, shapes, and even their tissues, they record changing environments, cultural values, social relationships, and notions of the sacred. For more than three years I was immersed in a study of live oaks in Louisiana and ceibas in Guatemala (see Map 1). Both of these trees are large and long-lived species that can appear as permanent fixtures in the landscape. My goal was to answer a few basic questions: How did these two trees come to be so important in their respective landscapes? How have people affected the trees and how, in turn, have the trees affected their human companions? It has been a fascinating and eye-opening journey into the topic of nature, culture, and the development of landscapes, one that is far from over.

The story of ceibas and live oaks is part of a much larger story of human relationships with what we call (collectively) nature. I believe

1.2 Oak Alley, on the Mississippi River in Louisiana, is a symbol of the antebellum plantation era.

Map 1.1 Study areas: Louisiana and Guatemala

that in interactions with trees, *Homo sapiens'* closest counterpart in the plant kingdom, humans express fundamental relationships with the nonhuman that help define who we are. The dividing line between humans and trees can become thin. As John Evelyn put it in the seventeenth century, "What is homo but *arbor inversa?*" Thus people have married trees, condemned them for murder, and given them legal standing. Trees in children's literature love to give advice. The wise "ents" in J. R. R. Tolkien's *The Lord of the Rings* series even manage to walk. In Thailand, Buddhist monks have amazed Westerners by wrapping trees in robes and ordaining them as monks in order to promote conservation efforts in a way that makes sense there. Plenty of cultural groups claim descent from particular species of trees.[1]

Big trees, those that have survived many human generations, play an important role in the structure of landscapes and the experience of place. Few are neutral in their meaning. They can reflect cultural identity, notions of the sacred, concepts of nature, and individual or group memory. A single massive baobab in the flat, dry landscape of sub-Saharan Africa says something entirely different from a row of columnar poplars along a road in France, or the tangled labyrinth of aerial roots and branches of a sprawling banyan in India. The baobab means water, shelter, familiar guide, and nourishment for nearby villagers and weary travelers. Poplars mark travel routes, too, but are not centers, like the baobab; instead, they imply movement, borders, a manicured landscape of tidy fields where edges matter. A single banyan can shelter an entire market, provide room for play, harbor holy men and women in silent meditation, and draw pilgrims from miles away for worship. Learning to decipher trees' messages is an exercise in natural and cultural history.

Humans come from a long line of arboreal primates. At one time, trees furnished just about everything for life—shelter, food, medicine, tools, clothing, and travel routes. Talking about trees was so important that names for trees are among the earliest words in the Proto–Indo European language. Besides their role in subsistence, trees are intimately tied to notions of the sacred. Through much of the world, they have been recognized as home for a variety of gods and spirits. Individual trees, certain species as a whole, and chosen groves are important places in the landscape for ritual practices, community gatherings, or private mediation.[2]

People and trees working together have created distinctive landscapes all over the world. In highland Spain and Portugal and on the rolling hills of California, separate peoples developed stable oak woodlands by managing native stands for acorn production. On the Iberian Peninsula the system includes feeding pigs on the abundant acorns; in California, the nutritious acorns were a major staple crop, managed in part by fire. Both olive groves, featuring gnarled old trees with their silver-green foliage, and deep green shady cypress walks have been part of Mediterranean landscapes for millennia. England has centuries-old coppiced woodlands, ancient root systems that bring forth ever-new saplings for house construction, and that harbor carpets of colorful spring wildflowers. Pollarded willows with enormous trunks and bushy heads of new shoots line rivers in Europe, their roots holding the banks, their tops harvested and twisted into baskets by people. Before disease claimed New England's famous elms in the twentieth century, settlers of European descent had created a region known for its beautiful villages and roads shaded by the spreading, graceful canopies of American elms. Now they've been replaced in the popular imagination by century-old maple trees that yield syrup in spring, and blaze red and orange each fall, attracting tourists by the millions. Management of native plants for basketry, food, and other uses has profoundly affected extensive regions, so that it becomes more and more difficult to distinguish between "natural" and "cultural" parts of the landscape.[3]

Also adding to the complexity of landscapes is the human proclivity to move plants around with them. What was once considered "exotic" can become a "natural" part of the scene. England's familiar sycamores were introduced into that country only at the end of the sixteenth century. The classic English hedgerows, and their well-loved elms, were also human creations of a particular time period; nevertheless, when the elms (many of them imports from mainland Europe) succumbed to disease in the twentieth century, their loss was mourned as a national tragedy. Across the Atlantic, in the prairie region of the American Midwest, settlers planted small square forests of eastern trees around homesteads to keep the great open spaces at bay. They soon became a normal part of the scene. English settlers transformed great stretches of New Zealand when they tamed these open spaces by planting miles of hedges, using familiar trees and shrubs from home.[4]

The story of the yews in English cemeteries is a good example of how one generation of planters can affect the landscape for centuries, even millennia. In *The Churchyard Yew and Immortality*, the English geographer Vaughn Cornish traced the origins of the familiar brooding, dark green giants that stand next to so many village churches. Using old land and church records, correspondence with parish vicars, and his own observations, he came to some surprising conclusions. Although yews today are associated mostly with druids, he found that it was Norman Christian missionaries moving up through England in the eleventh century who planted them. They used this sole native English evergreen to substitute for cypress, the usual choice for Mediterranean burial grounds. Many of today's trees date to the eleventh century, making them nearly one thousand years old. Cornish observed that people still repeat the customary planting patterns, not knowing why they do it—it just looks and feels right.

Trees, as living things, take an active part in these transformations. Some have a particular talent for adapting to life with people. Tropical oranges, when brought to Italy and France, required glass houses to survive, but in Paraguay they fairly leapt from the confines of gardens to invade the native flora and soon seemed native themselves. Apples did the same in New England; they are now welcomed as a familiar friend in old pastures and even managed as an important wildlife food source in regrown forests. Eucalyptus trees from Australia, planted all over the world, including California and the Andean highlands, have succeeded in populating the world beyond their wildest dreams. The huge trees, with their blue-gray foliage and distinctive odor, dominate parts of these landscapes, and manage to keep competition at bay. The ginkgo, too, must be grateful. From its early role as a captive of temple gardens in China, it has become an enormously widespread ornamental in cities worldwide. Its wild relations, meanwhile, have gone extinct. In addition, the ginkgo is revered today as a miraculous source of energy and well-being. As dispersal agents, humans have done well by these species.[5]

Among the most admired trees of the world are those that manage to achieve great size and age. Identifying and recording such trees is a long-standing human interest. John Evelyn recorded the giants of England in his seventeenth-century *Silva*. A current-day counterpart is Thomas Packenham, who has described sixty "remarkable" British trees, most of them extremely large and/or old. Among them is the "Great chestnut" by the church of Tortworth in England, believed to date to the twelfth century, and still a massive tree. In North America, the discovery of giant sequoias and redwoods in the western Sierras in the nineteenth century led to pilgrimages to the "sacred groves" of California. After scientists publicized the age of California's bristle cone pines, trees that, though not huge, are able to live for up to five thousand years, people began to pay tribute to these wind-blown survivors in the Sierras. In Mexico, Montezuma's cypress, remnant of pre-conquest gardens outside of Oaxaca, draws visitors, as do several ancient ginkgos in South Korea and China. Other trees believed to reach one thousand years of age include the tatara, sacred among the Maori of New Zealand; the monkey puzzle, source of food and also sacred among the Pehuenche of Chile and Argentina; baobabs of Africa; and the cumaru (producer of aromatic tonka beans) of the Amazon region.[6]

Organizations to protect and celebrate big old trees are publishing directories and books and leading trips to visit them. In the United States, we have national, state, and local groups that track so-called champion—largest individual specimens of particular species—trees and famous and historic trees. It is even possible to buy descendants of specific famous individuals, and someone has recently decided to preserve tissue from the biggest of the big to make sure the genetic material is not lost.[7]

Why so much focus on big and old trees? One reason is that trees have a long history among human societies as images of cosmic order. Different kinds of trees have symbolized life, fertility, community, and the world's sacred center. Yggdrasil, a giant ash tree, formed the center of the Norse cosmos, the *axis mundi*, its branches reaching into the sky, its roots to the underworld. In India, the Pipal, or bhodi tree, is venerated as the tree under which the Buddha was enlightened (although its history as a sacred tree is much older). The oak of Guernica, a specific living tree (although it has been replanted several times) is the symbolic center of the Basque people today. Other species have symbolized the center in different times and places. Psychologist Carl Jung focused on trees as important symbols of transformation in dreams. He also linked them to images of the cross, which he interpreted as symbolizing the tree of life, and the archetypal mother, in several different cultures.[8]

As symbols of the center, specific living trees in the landscape sometimes take on a sacred character. Yet usually it is not the trees themselves that are objects to be worshipped; rather, they are the place where the sacred world can break through into human reality, where communication with the gods is possible. The bodhi tree at Bodh Gaya in India, for instance, has been a pilgrimage site for more than two thousand years. A visitor in the seventh century described it as surrounded by a brick wall, and with a stone altar below its branches. (This tree has been replanted several times over the centuries, but that does not seem to detract.) Certain tree places, either individual trees or groves, are thus set aside, declared separate, off limits, different from the ordinary or profane. People will forego material gain to protect such trees, and mourn trees that are damaged or killed.[9]

As a number of critical studies have shown, the symbolism of particular trees has been used by the powerful to assert their control over land and people. In Georgian England, the elite class manipulated landscape trees and woodlands to maintain their power and make the existing social order look natural. Species like the oak, which were equated with great families, as well as ash and elm, were off limits to the lower classes. Fortunately, meanings can also be subverted. During the American Revolutionary War the aristocratic oaks became liberty trees.[10] Also important to remember, when analyzing the meaning of trees, especially in the past, are the voices of people who lived amid the trees. While the aristocracy was moving mature oaks around on their country estates to perfect their views, what of the spreading village trees around which people gathered and children played, trees that meant home and community? The landscape, as geographer Yi-Fu Tuan has continued to show, is full of hidden dimensions, experienced by people on many levels and in different ways depending on their own cultural and personal backgrounds. Like other landscape elements, trees can evoke fear, joy, comfort, mystery, sorrow, tradition, and childhood.[11] Their many and varied roles are what make them such rich subjects for research and insight into the experience of place and landscape.

Another explanation for the tree fixation of humans is biological and evolutionary. The theory of biophilia, for instance, suggests that humans have an innate, genetically programmed need to affiliate with other living organisms. Often humans choose large, charismatic species on which to focus this need. Based in evolutionary reasoning is Jay Appleton's notion that when looking at landscapes, humans consider "prospect and refuge," an instinctive remnant of survival in a savanna environment. An attractive (safe, desirable) landscape has a balance of both—places to be concealed, with good views to survey the surrounding landscape for prey and predators. A single large tree provides both. Within its shade, where survival is temporarily not the main preoccupation, creative and community activities can take place. Such trees, then, become places in the landscape with great significance.[12]

For urban dwellers, parks and street plantings often provide the main contact with trees. The whole notion of city trees is actually relatively recent. Beginning in the eighteenth century, there was a movement to green streets and squares because trees were thought to make the environment healthier and improve the character of inhabitants. This was especially true in Europe; the custom came later to the more recently colonized North American continent, and was by no means universal. Today, however, urban forests (a term that would have seemed absurd not that long ago) are threatened by high levels of pollution, random damage from vehicles, overhead interference with wires, and root crowding. Tree life expectancy is quite short. And yet many people, regardless of the impracticality, still want big trees planted in the city.[13]

There may be good reasons for this. Recent studies on children's relationships with nature suggest that interactions with trees can help shape concepts of self. Trees are among the crucial places where children can explore, develop physical skills, hide out, learn about seasonal changes, and make private spaces to just be. That has certainly been borne out in my presentations on trees to various audiences. Anytime I show an image of children climbing in trees, or of tree houses, or even a few rungs nailed to a tree, people smile and sigh. Given the opportunity, they tell tales of climbing, hiding, playing, and dreaming in favorite trees. They remember smells, the texture of the ground beneath, sounds of wind in the leaves, picking up things that dropped from the branches, the feel of bark. Emotional memories are vivid as are the physical sensations experienced in and around these tree places.[14]

The two tree species I chose to study are the ceiba (*Ceiba pentandra* [L.] Gaertn.) of Guatemala and the live oak (*Quercus virginiana* Miller) of Louisiana. Ceibas interested me because there was some mystery about their distribution pattern, and because of their reputation as a sacred tree since ancient times. Live oaks were the dominant street tree in southern Louisiana and clearly had a symbolic role connected to plantations and Southern life in general. Although not related botanically, the two trees have some important things in common. Both are among the largest and longest-lived trees in their areas, and neither is valued for an economic product today. Both are the subject of many stories and legends, and both have affected their landscapes physically and symbolically. Both appeared to have been taken beyond their native range by people, but just how and when and by whom was unclear.

A cross-cultural comparison promised to yield more depth into the question of trees and landscapes than looking at only one example. Such an approach triggers questions and comparisons that can yield new insights and different points of view.[15] To help with focus, since both these trees cover tremendous areas, I decided to limit the study areas geographically to Louisiana and Guatemala.

As it turns out, the two areas also share some qualities. Both had thriving indigenous cultures before the European invasions in the 1500s. Both feature rich biotic diversity. Plantation agriculture and export crops, including sugar and cotton, followed colonialization, and are still important exports from both. Topographically the two are quite different. Louisiana is mostly flat, while Guatemala, except for coastal lowlands, is largely mountainous. Although both areas were colonized by Europeans (who created the political boundaries that define each place today), Guatemala was first settled primarily by Spanish, Louisiana by successive waves of Spanish-, English-, and French-speaking peoples. In Guatemala the major cultural groups today are the Spanish-speaking Ladinos and the native Mayans, with a smaller proportion of African and Asian-derived groups. Louisiana is known primarily for its Southern white culture, French-speaking Cajuns, a large population of African Americans and smaller percentages of other groups.

My goal was to learn what these trees were doing in each place, and how humans and trees together create landscapes. I wanted to understand the relationships from both sides—the people and the trees. Methods were borrowed from several traditions, including cultural geography and ethnobotany. The focus was on the individual, specific, and observable, from which I could draw conclusions about more general patterns. Because so much depends on the trees' part in this, I spent a lot of time learning their natural history (see Chapter 3), relying on published sources and information gleaned from interviews and observations. The approach that proved most useful for fieldwork was ethnography.

Ethnographic methods, traditionally used by anthropologists to study culture, can also be applied to understanding the nature of place and the experience of landscape.[16] Following accepted practices, I watched and recorded everyday interactions with the study trees, and spoke with people from all walks of life about ceibas and live oaks. The topic of trees was nonthreatening. In fact, it led to many animated conversations and elicited all sorts of stories and memories. Interviews varied in format, from structured formal interactions in offices of experts to more casual conversations on buses and sidewalks, in plazas, restaurants, and other public and private places. Originally, I hoped that measuring trunks would help me determine the age of trees, but it turned out that both these species grow at highly variable rates. Establishing age and growth rate requires repeated measurements over a period of years. Instead, measuring trees was a sure way to attract people and engage them in conversation. Photographs recorded landscape roles, branching patterns, and comparisons between the two species. I also gathered images from postcards, artwork, tourist promotions, and archival sources.

Analyzing ethnographic interviews and observations is different from the task of calculating means and standard deviations. My goal has been to allow the people and trees to speak, through their actions, words, and presence in the landscape. That meant slowly developing categories and identifying patterns, then going back to the field to check them out. Eventually, as I pieced together firsthand observations with evidence from interviews and historic material, the stories presented in this book evolved. They are not the only stories, merely the ones I found, or that found me. Others wait to be told.

Human-tree relationships provide a window into the whole topic of nature and culture. For some time, geographers and others have struggled to refine our notions of these two terms. Are they separate concepts, as has generally been accepted? Or is everything we know culture, including the cultural notion of nature? Or is culture something nature has produced (and thus is part of it)? Some scholars have suggested we drop the duality and speak instead of nature-culture hybrids, or put them together into one term, "nature/culture," that better expresses the reality of our world.[17] I don't propose to resolve these questions. Rather, I believe the details of how ceibas and live oaks, together with people, have created distinctive landscapes and places, offer insights into what actually goes on between humans and the other-than-human. From that, perhaps we can infer something larger regarding the concepts of nature and culture.

On a more immediate, practical level, I hope this work proves useful to those who make decisions regarding trees in our landscapes. What people revealed about live oaks and ceibas is not limited to those species. Wherever there are trees, there is a dimension of meaning that is difficult to gauge from casual observation. The species and particular individuals hold great power. The results of removing, modifying, or planting trees can be profound and long-lasting. It is worth the time spent to learn, watch, and listen.

Chapter 2

DANCES WITH TREES

NOTES FROM THE FIELD

A FULL-GROWN *Ceiba pentandra* is hard to miss: wrinkled gray ele-phant-skin bark covers a thick trunk up to thirty-five feet or more in circumference (Fig. 2.1). Small, fierce thorns bristle here and there on trunk and branches. Enormous buttressed roots splay out in all directions, merging into the trunk a good ten feet above the ground. Above, fat branches angle skyward in contorted patterns, or form a series of horizontal whorls of three, regularly spaced along a trunk that can be two hundred feet tall. Some of the taller ceibas have only a tuft of greenery crowning a bare columnar trunk; others are more squat, with widely spreading branches that cast generous shade.

Live oaks, too, are unmistakable. The huge, gnarly trees form dark green islands in the flat Louisiana landscape. Up close, their small, oval, leathery leaves don't look much like those of northern oaks. Masses of ferns cascade down the dark, furrowed bark. Low-growing, twisting branches make them much more inviting to climb than the forbidding ceibas (Fig. 2.2). Although they can grow tall in the forest, their more familiar shape is that of an open-crowned, spreading hulk, draped with tangles of gray Spanish moss, with a shadow that can measure 150 feet across.

Face to face with a huge old tree, the human body feels frail and ephemeral. No wonder people's reactions to such trees range from worship to fear, great affection to hatred. Over their lifetimes, ceibas and live oaks interact with many generations of humans, bearing evidence of these relationships in how and where they have grown and the kinds of places they help create.

2.1 *Fat ceiba trunks bristling with spines can soar hundreds of feet toward the sky.*

2.2 Massive, low, spreading branches of live oaks invite climbing.

My first challenge in studying these trees was to let go of cultural and personal assumptions about both species. The big ones, and those in famous places, instantly draw attention. But the landscape contains many more that are younger and not so remarkable in appearance. Learning to see these took time and patience, and a willingness to be led by the people of both regions. Also crucial was listening carefully to the stories told by people who lived and worked with the trees, and comparing what they said to what they did. Some experts taught me how to "read" the trees to find out more about their condition and history. The process was like watching a photograph develop: first the major forms and shapes became visible; slowly the finer details filled in. Much was and still is hidden. Offered here are examples from fieldwork that convey some of the essential aspects of relationships with ceibas and live oaks in contemporary Guatemala and Louisiana. How these relationships came to be is further examined in the following chapters.

CEIBA

Initial research in the literature indicated ceibas were typical of plazas, the physical and symbolic center of villages and cities throughout Latin America. It was known as the World Tree of the Maya and as the official national tree of Guatemala.

My first encounter with the ceiba of Palín (see Chapter 1) fulfilled all expectations: Mayan people, plaza, market, church, native languages, and a huge tree at the center of it all. That visit, though, was also marked by sensory overload. Loud music, shouting and laughter, a riot of bright colors, pungent odors, constant movement, and unfamiliar words overwhelmed and hid the subtler details of this place. It was only after repeated visits, and a full day there from dawn to dusk, that I began to appreciate how this tree and its human neighbors, together, create this place (see Map 2.1).

Ceiba Places

Early in the morning, just past dawn, the market area is quiet, as a few young girls remove bright blue plastic sheeting that protects the stalls at night. Close to the trunk, two women dish out *atole*, a steaming hot maize gruel, into bowls and cups. Customers sit on the steps of the massive cement structure that surrounds the tree. Girls play and joke with each other and their younger siblings, some eating breakfast as they begin their daily routine. The ground under the tree is remarkably clean, kept that way by constant sweeping.

The plaza is a mixture of private space—an extension of home—and public place, where community relationships are played out (Fig. 2.3). The *vendedoras*, who sell fresh fruits and vegetables, dried and prepared foods and flowers, are the Poqomam-speaking women of Palín. Their place is the south side of the tree, where they have permanent stalls. Women and families from Santa María de Jesús, the next village up on the flanks of the volcano Agua, spread their more temperate produce on blankets on the north side of the tree. Outsiders from Guatemala City, including men who sell books, clothing, and dry goods, fit here and there, mostly at the outer edge

2.3 Beneath the shade of Palín's village ceiba, social dramas and cycles unfold continuously.

of the tree's branches, and in neighboring tin-roofed shacks. *Ladino* (Spanish-speaking) women from Palín come to buy produce, often from their favorite *vendedora*. By mid-morning trade is brisk.

The market is the village's gossip center; news spreads quickly from stall to stall. The tree also brings contact with the outside world. People come to Palín for two main reasons: to buy or sell at the market and to see the famous tree. Guatemalans from the nearby capital often combine shopping and fun. Families stop on their way to the coast, to sit in the shade and eat while the children run around the tree and read the signs at its base. One family from Antigua, who took me to Palín for my first visit, considered it a fine Sunday outing, following the visit with a trip to the nearby hot springs. Foreigners are infrequent—this is not on the regular tourist route. There are no hotels in Palín. Strangers must leave at the end of the day unless they have a friend in town.

Years ago, I was told, the road ran right through town; buses and cars would stop next to the tree. Now it is closed to traffic. Visitors have to walk from where the bus lets them off on the highway, or park their cars along side streets. Stalls are arranged and oriented in relation to the tree. Those not buying or selling tend to sit or stand either facing the tree from the plaza edges or church steps, looking in, or on the cement structure that surrounds the tree, looking out.

The women don't say much about the tree to me. One tells me it was planted by *los antepasados*. Two old men standing on the steps of the church report it is 450 years old. Its massive roots, which are breaking the cement structure that surrounds the tree, have grown into the church basement. Eileen Maynard, an anthropologist who lived in Palín for several years in the 1960s, heard the story of the ceiba's *nahual*. This spirit is a fat white woman in a white dress who planted the ceiba years ago and now, being fond of motoring, rides on the hoods of cars that stop under the tree.[1] A young boy from Santa María de Jesús who attached himself to me as a guide was happy to confirm that an enormous and fearsome *culebra* (snake) also lives in the tree. Conversations with several women drew anecdotes about small, harmless snakes that occasionally fall from the branches. A few years go, a vendedora put up the large pigeon house perched high in the tree. Sometimes women look up from their work to watch the white birds flutter among the tree's massive branches. The tin-roofed shacks that border the plaza, extending the market, are blazing hot on this sunny day.

Mid-afternoon, clouds move in and it starts to rain. Without its leaves, the ceiba catches only the first round of drops. From beneath a huge branch, I watch as the plaza clears quickly. Vendors efficiently cover their wares and move into the shelter of surrounding roofs, repeating a well-rehearsed routine. After a while, the rain stops. By then it is just about time to quit and people begin to clean up. On the north side, the empty plaza becomes a basketball court. The stalls on the south remain covered but untended, safe beneath the tree.

Even in this apparently idyllic setting, though, the reality of violence in Guatemala intrudes. One day in 1994, on the official Día del Ejército (Day of the Army), the plaza suddenly bristled with soldiers. It was unsettling, seeing men in uniform carrying rifles, moving restlessly through the crowd, in pairs or singly, staring suspiciously. Although one occasionally stopped to buy something, the soldiers were generally ignored, as if they inhabited a separate world.

Tree-shaded marketplaces like that of Palín are scarce today; the only other one confirmed by recent visitors was in the town of Sacapulas, where two old ceibas still shade the market. Escuintla, just west of Palín, used to have a market under a famous large ceiba.

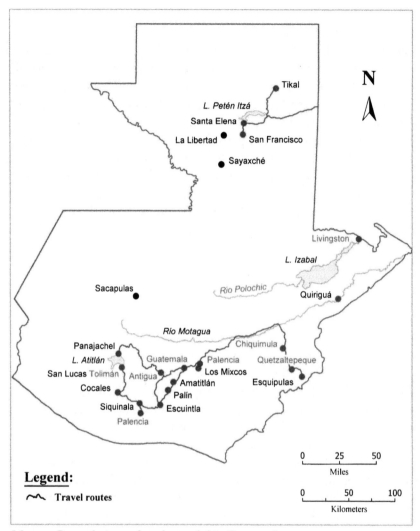

Map 2.1 Research sites and roads traveled in Guatemala

When the town's *alcalde* (mayor) had it removed some years ago, many residents were angry. An agricultural expert employed by the state told me one version of the story. The alcalde, he said, wanted to refurbish and modernize the plaza. But cutting down a ceiba requires government permission. So a story was circulated that a branch of the tree had fallen, killing ten people. That was enough to get the permit. Whether or not the deaths actually happened is unclear (others reported it as fact). The ceiba, however, is definitely gone. I hopped off a bus in Escuintla after one of the Palín visits and went in search of the plaza. The city is a relatively large one that lies in the *tierra caliente*, or tropical climate zone. It is an important commercial and trade center, situated where the major travel route along the Pacific crosses the road from Guatemala City to the coast. The plaza was hot and sunny, not a place to linger that day. Trimmed small shrubs edged diagonal paved paths lined with benches. A few people sat on benches, while others tended several food carts, but there was none of the bustling, colorful activity of Palín. There was no center, no focal point around which people could orient themselves.

Another bus carried me northwest along La Costa, the flat, Pacific lowlands where vast plantations produce sugar and cotton for export. Squeezed into the packed bus, perched on my backpack in the center isle, but held up by the people on either side, I counted ceibas. Within the fields, they stand out, gawky but distinctive, stark remnants of forests that once covered the plains. The Maya won't cut ceibas, I had read and been told countless times. Besides, laws now prohibit cutting the national tree. Ceibas also show up on the road margins. Once we stopped at a police checkpoint, and sure enough, the uniformed men had their shelter under a ceiba, this one with painted trunk. Later, dividing my numbers, rough as they were, it turned out there was an average of one ceiba per kilometer visible from the bus between Escuintla and Cocales.

My destination that afternoon was La Democracia, my quarry a tree I suspected of being a ceiba. It was pictured in a travel guide as the backdrop for an outdoor collection of "Olmecoid" heads. These are large, relatively crude basalt carvings that resemble ancient sculptures from the Veracruz area of Mexico. Getting to this small settlement meant leaving the highway to catch a smaller local bus south. On the way, we passed several magnificent ceibas standing tall among the sugarcane fields. A young woman, carrying bags of produce and fresh eggs back from the market, took an interest in my obsession and directed me to the town plaza when we got off the bus.

The ceiba of La Democracia presides over a relatively large plaza. Surrounding it are the church, town offices, and some commercial establishments, including a restaurant. One part of this open area displays the large stone heads, arranged in rows; formal plantings, paths, and a basketball hoop with playing area occupy the rest.

2.4 *Structures around ceiba trees come in all sizes and shapes. This most elaborate one, featuring red, yellow, and blue paint, is in La Democracia, on the Pacific coastal lowlands.*

Except for the heads, the basic elements were familiar. The ceiba tree, though, was surrounded by a remarkable structure that prevented the usual tape measure trick.

Sitting in an open-air eatery, sipping a cold drink in a vain effort to get cool (at 165 m elevation, this place is always hot and humid), I focused on the structure, easily the most elaborate I'd seen. Made of concrete, it totally surrounded the tree with a series of steps, a flat area for walking backed by a circular bench, and, above, a flat roof. It was painted in brilliant shades of red, yellow, and blue. Behind it, the ceiba's trunk was painted white. What was the reason for all this effort? Was it to show off the tree? To protect the tree? Or to protect people? The roof might be to keep out rain or sun, or maybe snakes or bird droppings.

Hardly anyone was moving in the oppressive heat and brilliant sunshine of early afternoon. A few old men sat under the tree, talking, and one shoe-shine boy was busy. Once a line of tired-looking men, their clothes sweaty and dirty, walked by slowly on the far side of the plaza, probably sugarcane workers, returning from the fields. A few children played with a ball among the old heads. Later, a couple of young men were shooting basketballs. I wondered what it would be like here at other times, but for once there were few people to ask.

These structures around ceiba trees began to fascinate me. Almost all the ceibas in plazas had some kind of enclosure. They ranged from the very simple—a circle of white stones—to this multilayered one at La Democracia. Many were raised above ground level, and clearly put in after the tree had been in place a long time. According to the frequent plaques identifying the national tree and giving dates of construction, along with names of those responsible, they were relatively recent projects, most dating to the last forty years.

How many other settlements in this region have such big ceibas? According to fellow travelers on buses, there are or were many, often on private plantations, the population centers in this area. They acted as gathering places and landmarks, associated with and named for the places where they grew, whether town or plantation. Several times men told me with pride that their grandfather or other relative had planted a particular ceiba.

My day ended up in the highlands, on the shore of Lake Atitlán, after a hair-raising bus ride up the south flank of the volcanic ridge. This is rough country, with roads that wash out regularly, and fierce fighting over land rights. The road we traveled had been off the bus route for some time because of *la violencia*. Glimpses of ceibas became scarcer as we ascended through several climatic zones to the welcome coolness of the mountains. Night was falling as we pulled into San Lucas Tolimán, a quiet town across the lake from Panajachel, the famous tourist mecca.

Much to my surprise, next to the nearly empty and not quite finished "hotel" on the lakeshore where I found a room was a ceiba. Not a very old one, nor marked in any way, yet definitely a ceiba. The owner had nothing to say about it. Women and children of the town who came to the shore to wash as darkness fell seemed oblivious of the tree. It was strangely close to the new walls of the building.

At dawn, from the early ferry, I looked back at the ceiba's familiar shape looming through the mist next to an almost-full moon setting beyond it. When asked, the ferryman explained that the mayor of the town had planted it in honor of the annual Día del Árbol, the

Day of the Tree. What sort of role will it play in this town, what stories will people tell about it in the future?

Ceibas as Markers

Actually, I shouldn't have been so surprised at finding that ceiba. Ceibas had been dodging my path in the highlands ever since my arrival. Not massive or famous like the Palín tree, they formed part of a different class of ceibas, known to far fewer people. Nevertheless, for those who know, they are important elements of the landscape.

Antigua Guatemala was my home base. This city of about fifty thousand is 1,530 meters elevation, about 40 km southwest of Guatemala City, in a valley surrounded by three prominent volcanoes. From the 1540s to the 1770s it was the capital of New Spain. When repeated earthquakes forced relocation of the capital, Antigua remained as a quieter, colonial-style city with an international feel. Now it is a popular destination for foreigners wanting to attend Spanish language schools. Walking the colorful, cobbled streets, one hears not only Spanish, but Mayan, English, German, French, Chinese, and many other languages. All around the city, in the surrounding hills, are smaller villages, largely Mayan, where milpas and dooryard gardens are still an essential part of life.

My Spanish teacher, Juana, took an immediate interest in the topic of ceibas and announced there were several right in town. That's how we ended up ringing the doorbell at Dr. Edwin Shook's house on 5a Avenida one evening and interrupting his supper. Shook is an American archeologist who was among the earliest interpreters of the ruins of Tikal. Juana had shown me the ceiba at the Hotel Santo Domingo, growing unceremoniously squashed against a wall. The elegant hotel had once been Shook's home (and a monastery before that). Our exchange was brief. Although startled, he was gracious enough to answer a few questions. He had planted the tree, yes. It came from the lowlands, of course (where else?). He planted it because he liked ceibas and he was just sorry he'd put it so close to the wall. It grew much faster than he'd expected.

Other ceibas soon followed. Next to Antigua is Jocotenango. Juana led me to a ceiba planted in the median strip in front of the church, part of the town's plaza. I had walked right by this tree sev-

2.5 *Standing in front of the ceiba he remembers planting twelve years earlier, this man is worried that its growth point has been destroyed by vandals. Note the regular branching pattern of three branches along trunk.*

eral years earlier, following a Palm Sunday procession from Antigua that ended at the church. (Back then, I was blissfully unaware of ceibas.) Many residents are equally oblivious, including another Spanish teacher at our school who passed the tree every day. It was disconcerting to find several Mayan women who looked at me strangely when I asked them what kind of tree that was. No idea, they said. ("Some sacred tree," I thought.)

The town office and library were closed. Juana, though, was persistent and finally found someone who could tell us about the tree: the man who was patiently sweeping the plaza (Fig. 2.5). He told us quietly that he had planted the tree, a gift to the town from the mayor of another town. He felt a certain responsibility for its well-being. As we looked at the tree in more detail he showed us how vandals had climbed up and damaged the central growth point. Clearly upset, he was concerned the tree would not grow any more. The ceiba's age became a matter of controversy. A well-dressed woman noticed us talking about the tree and came over to find out what was going on. She was quite sure the tree had been planted twenty years earlier, no matter how often our original source repeated quietly, keeping his eyes on the ground, that it was just twelve years ago.

Another adventure with Juana was to her hometown, San Juan del Obispo. The elaborate colonial home built for the first bishop of the region is now inhabited by nuns who wear the full, black habit. (Local residents affectionately call them *los pingüinos*, the penguins). The first ceiba grew at the entrance to town, by the bus stop. It didn't look like much, with its small stature and scarred trunk marked with a red painted arrow. Juana told me that the men who planted this tree wrote their names on a piece of paper that is buried beneath its roots. She remembered wanting to climb it as a child. We paid a young boy to climb up and get a single pod amid the branches. Although the foliage was that of a ceiba, as Juana described the flowers it bore, it became clear this must be *C. aesculifolia*, not *C. pentandra* (see Chapter 3). A year later, on a second visit, the tree's top branches had been chopped back by a work crew clearing the roadside for electric wires.

The second "ceiba" was younger, but much taller. It was growing near the *pila*—a communal cement basin common in Guatemalan villages, where women get water and wash clothes. The tree had been planted a few years earlier by a man who lived nearby. It was growing rapidly, possibly because of abundant water supplied by a leak in the waterline next to it. Both these ceibas (as identified by residents) are clearly in public spaces, not private back yards. Awareness of their presence and significance varies tremendously.

Acting on a tip from two Mayan girls who visited our school one day, we went up to San Antonio Aguas Calientes to search for a ceiba on the *cumbre*, or hill, that overlooks the small valley. We finally found a small, abject ceiba surrounded by grasses and weeds. Planted during a beautification project led by schoolchildren several years earlier, it bore the marks of machetes and nibbling animals. A year later it was gone, a victim of road building. Nobody I spoke with seemed overly concerned.

My host family in Antigua, meanwhile, were amused by my obsession and soon dubbed me a "ceibólogo." They began to ask others for information on famous trees and announced new finds at dinner. As an official ceibologo, I felt comfortable asking just about anyone for information on ceibas. One day, a young man in my neighborhood astonished me by saying there was a ceiba practically next door, in the next *colonia* (neighborhood). Doubtful but curious, I followed him down the street to a tree with an elaborate engraved metal sign, mounted on cement, announcing that Maximiliano Najero Mejicanos planted this ceiba in 1965 "with love for his country and his neighborhood." The tree grew right by the sidewalk, bordered by two homes and the street. Beyond it was an open area with grass and a playground, a sort of miniature plaza. The ground around the tree was smoothed and bare, popular with children who played marbles and other games. The tree itself didn't look too great, with several broken branches and marks on the trunk. Two women arriving home from market looked at me curiously, and when I asked who took care of the tree, they shrugged and laughed, saying, "Dios cuida a la ceiba" (God takes care of the ceiba).

Several days later a group of girls in school uniforms walked by me as I was returning home, each holding a potted baby tree. They had just been at a class learning how to plant trees, they told me, and when I asked about ceibas they said there was one at their school. The secretary at the school clearly thought me odd, but got permission for me to photograph the tree. It looked nothing like a valued sacred or national tree. It was surrounded by construction materials from renovations in progress, with planks and tools leaning against

2.6 Children attending this school in San Antonio Aguas Calientes were proud of their two ceiba trees.

the trunk. How long before it outgrows this space, I wondered, and how many other ceibas are hiding all over the place?

Three more ceibas soon popped up in San Antonio Aguas Calientes (the town with the sad little ceiba on the hill). A helpful man on a bicycle told me there were two at the evangelical school where he was custodian (Fig. 2.6). Wandering the dusty streets, I eventually spotted the fenced-in front yard with its two trees. A bicycle leaned against one, and two children were chasing each other around the other. Several students proudly identified the trees as ceibas. The custodian lived with his family in a small hut at the end of the school building. Beyond was his milpa. We sat for a while in the smoky hut, as his wife made tortillas and their children watched and listened. At first, he told me, the children had objected to having anything planted in their play area, but now they were proud of these trees they learned about in school. He showed me schoolbooks with illustrations of the national tree of Guatemala. On the way home, while waiting for a bus, I practically bumped into another young ceiba in the town of Santa Catarina, carefully planted in the town plaza within a cement-bordered square.

It turned out that planting ceiba trees at schools may have a long history. A middle-aged Ladino woman told me she remembered a big ceiba in the girls' school she attended in Guatemala City. Growing in a courtyard through which the students walked frequently, the tree created a quiet, shady place to read and rest between classes. She thought other schools had big ceibas, too, a natural part of these institutions.

Young ceibas can be tricky to identify. Once, while eating at Restaurant Asiole, on the highway near Amatitlán, I noticed a tree in the parking that looked like a possible ceiba. The restaurant owner was summoned. She assured me it was indeed a ceiba, one her husband had brought back from Venezuela. As she described the beautiful, large red flowers that covered the tree each year, it became clear this was most likely a kind of Bombax, a related genus often grown as an ornamental. We talked for some time about ceibas and their importance in Guatemala. Her husband had felt strongly about the national tree, she told me, and had once planted one and buried his name under it. She took up my cause and called around to find out if anyone knew about the ceiba of Amatitlán, in which I was interested. On a return visit a year later, I found the Asiole tree's cement edging had been painted bright yellow.

An obvious question that arose eventually was where the planted ceibas were coming from. When asked, people usually responded, "la costa." But where? Did they go to nurseries, or just find one somewhere and dig it up? I never saw anyone on a bus with a ceiba cradled in his or her lap. A nursery just outside of Antigua didn't have any. Finally, in Siquinala, a town on the Pacific coastal highway, I found some answers.

A nursery with a ceiba growing near the entrance seemed promising. When asked about the ceiba trees, the young man working there said they had two young ones, both of them beautiful. One was for sale. We walked between rows of nursery stock and potted plants

2.7 *Baby ceibas grow quickly; the one shooting straight up in center is only about a year old.*

of all kinds. Finally he pointed to a strapping baby ceiba leaning up against a plastic greenhouse. In its second year of growth, it was about eight feet tall, with tender green leaves, spines on the trunk, its roots bundled in plastic. After I had admired and photographed it, he wanted to show off another one, just because it was so *linda* (pretty). We wound our way through more paths, and into a field. The second ceiba, about the same size as the first, grew where it had sprouted, in the midst of rows of nursery stock (Fig. 2.7). It will stay there, he told me, because it is the national tree. The nursery owner and the manager were happy to talk. Not many people came to buy ceibas, they said. For shade trees, they recommend smaller species. Anyway, ceibas sprout on their own all over the lowlands. When the pods open, white silky cotton spills out, and wind spreads the small parachutes, each with a seed, until the ground is covered. At least some years. Other years, there are few or none. All he has to do is dig up a few trees for sale. Occasionally people from the highlands will come to buy a ceiba. Just a year or two ago, several soldiers had come and bought two ceibas to plant at a military base in the mountains.

Ceibas Lost and Found

One of my goals was to track down as many historically famous ceiba trees as possible to find out how they were doing. My list evolved from written accounts and interviews. It was surprisingly difficult to find out about specific trees. Alfonso Arivillaga, a Guatemalan anthropologist, was especially knowledgeable and generous with his time and suggestions. He described a famous ceiba tree in the town of Livingston, on the Atlantic coast. The people of this community are the Garifuna, or Black Caribs, whose traditions are a mix of African and American Indian origins. The ceiba grows in the cemetery, and is believed to harbor a large snake. It is a place of great power. Other trees he knew of included some on my list. The ceiba of Jocotenango (part of Guatemala City) was gone, while several large ones in the Petén, including the one in San Francisco, were still growing. About the ceiba of Palencia, though, even he didn't know for sure.

The ceiba of Palencia is famous because of a gruesome story: the head of Serapio Cruz, a national hero, was hung from its branches in the late nineteenth century. Getting to Palencia meant a bus to Guatemala City, then two other buses into the surrounding mountains on narrow roads. Palencia is a small place. On the way into town, a helpful companion on the bus pointed out the church where the ceiba used to be. It had died some years ago, replaced by a double row of trees that now formed a shady walk. The town did have some ceibas, though, I was told. Indeed, the plaza had a number of ceiba or ceiba-like trees. I was examining the area around them for clues when a woman who lived nearby came over to explain that two were ceibas and two *pochotes*. I couldn't tell the difference. The trees, maybe fifteen to twenty years old, had circles of white stones around them and a few white-painted seats.

Along came two cheery men carrying a large basket filled with izote flowers. They stopped to chat and let me take a photo, explaining they were going down to the capital to sell this bounty harvested from a friend's land. Casually, they added that there were a couple of big ceibas in the next town, Los Mixcos. Hopping on another bus, I soon arrived there. Sure enough, in the wide open grassy area that marked the center of town stood two large ceibas (Fig. 2.8). Although their painted trunks measured almost the same circumference (28 ft. and 28 ft., 11 in.), one was tall, the other spreading. An elderly man wandered out as I was measuring and photographing. After a few minutes, he began to talk about the trees and kept going for well over an hour. He lived right there, had known these trees all his life, and remembered the ceiba of Palencia. Nobody had ever asked him about them before.

As he talked, he painted a picture of this place on the weekend, when hundreds of people would come from all around the mountainous region to play soccer here. All day they would take turns in tournaments, playing or resting in the shade of the two massive trees. The ground would be covered with people, he said, around each tree. A prominent man of the village, now dead, had planted the trees many years ago, and he pointed in the direction of the valley where he had gone to dig up the seedlings. As for the Palencia tree, he chuckled when he talked about the time he was hired to help build a cement structure around it. "I always wondered if that helped kill the tree," he said. We were so involved in talking I almost missed the last bus out.

2.8 *Los Mixcos, a small town in the mountains outside the capital, hosts gatherings around its huge ceibas on weekends, when people come for regional soccer matches.*

The Petén Lowlands

The final area to investigate was the Petén, home of the ancient Maya. The Petén lowlands of northern Guatemala are still remote and mysterious, requiring days of travel to reach by bus from the highlands. In the rainy season it's especially exciting since the roads tend to become sheer mud. Several airlines now make regular flights to Santa Elena, not far from the ruins of Tikal, and it is definitely the preferred travel mode for those who can afford it, especially foreigners.

From my hotel room in Santa Elena, home base for day trips to the ruins, I could see the town's plaza and resident ceiba tree (Fig. 2.9). The modern Catholic church is across one of the side streets. Easily the tallest growing thing in town, this ceiba is nevertheless relatively young, no more than twenty to thirty years old (and possibly younger). The plaza is small, mostly paved, and divided geometrically by paths. During the day a few children played there, with or without their mother. It tended to be quiet. But in the evening, the food stall set up next to the sidewalk under the tree was busy and lit up in bright colors. People stopped there to buy snacks and to chat or flirt with the young women who tended it. Young people sat along the main road, watching others walk by, drinking sodas and eating, laughing into the night. Just down the road was the *comedor* La Ceiba, a modest restaurant with a sign out front that featured the silhouette of a ceiba.

On the way to the ruins in a minivan early the next morning, the driver knew exactly which ceiba I wanted to stop and photograph— the one with oropendula nests. Oropendulas are tropical colony-nesting birds that look for trees with outstretched branches from which to hang their homes. Several hundred basket-like woven nests, shaped like elongated gourds, dangled from the high ceiba canopy, safe from predators (see Figure 3.3).

Tourists arriving at Tikal must walk through an open grassy area with scattered trees to get to the ruins. A number of the trees had signs tacked to them saying "Ceiba," although to my eye they did not look like ceibas. Francisco Cane Acosta, a naturalist guide native to that area, laughed when I asked him about those trees. No, they weren't ceibas, he told me. In his well-worn book on flora of the area he pointed to the genus *Bombax* as the probable identity. The fake ceibas were labeled for the tourists, who didn't know any better and like to see ceibas, he said. It helps identify this as a Mayan place.

On the path to the ruins there is one fine specimen of the ceiba, *C. pentandra*, identified and explained as the Mayan sacred tree on an accompanying sign. It has the typical huge buttresses and smooth gray bark. Compared to the ceibas in plazas, though, it is far more upright, its high branches casting very little shade on the ground. Within the ruins, ceibas were not evident. I couldn't help but remember Copán, a Mayan site in Honduras, just across the border from Guatemala. There, ceibas sprawled all over the crumbling pyramids, having taken root amid the rubble and grown into fantastic rambling shapes.

A few days later I was on the way to the town of San Francisco Petén. As usual, the ride was noisy, hot, and filled with good humor. Also as usual, the driver's seat and mirror were surrounded with crosses, images of Mary and Jesus, plastic flowers, trinkets, and prayers. With Latin music blaring, we bumped along the gravel road that led through pastures and patches of rainforest. Only a few people got off at San Francisco; one pointed me toward the prominent ceiba, a dark hulk in the middle of a large green expanse surrounded by dirt roads and brightly painted modest homes.

2.9 *In the lowlands of the Petén, Santa Elena's plaza sports a vigorous young ceiba.*

2.10 *Planted in 1828, the ceiba in San Francisco Petén, next to the Catholic church, is the town's dominant feature. The fenced area beneath the tree is used for community celebrations, like Carnaval.*

The tree seemed to grow as I walked toward it, completely dwarfing the little colonial-style church next to it. It was enclosed by a wood and wire fence that formed a rectangular enclosure, entered through a gate. Within was welcome shade. The only person in sight was the young man sweeping. Another man in his twenties, quick to see a potential customer, disappeared briefly and came back with a bundle wrapped in cloth that contained "old Mayan" items for sale, clearly either contraband or fake. He faded away when I explained my interest was only in the ceiba.

As I began the usual measuring routine, I wondered how to learn anything about the tree since the place seemed deserted. Soon several children appeared. Gradually their numbers grew until a small crowd was following me around. They all appeared to be Ladino— no signs of Mayan dress or language. When I expressed an interest in seeing twigs up close, they instantly began to hurl any object at hand into the branches to see what they could dislodge. Later they explained they'd had plenty of practice because they always tried to break the lights townspeople had fastened up there. Interacting physically with this tree does present a challenge. The buttresses are so massive that children, even adults, can easily hide among them. Climbing is impossible. Instead, the ceiba, with its fence, makes a defined place for community gatherings. The night before the town had celebrated Carnaval, they told me. That is the Latin American equivalent of Mardi Gras, the last big party before Lent begins.

As we examined leaves and twigs together, some of the children asked if their tree was bigger than the famous tree at Palín, far away to the south, that they had heard about. The Palín tree's trunk is slightly bigger in circumference. Other than that, the two are quite different. Palín is the only big tree, surrounded by gray pavement and buildings and people most of the time. Its branches are largely bare and gray. Color comes from the produce and clothing of Mayan women. The San Francisco tree stands within an expanse of lush green, and its branches are so loaded with a profusion of epiphytes that it looks like a garden itself. At mid-day it is a quiet place, protected, surrounded by a sleepy tropical town, few people in sight except the crowd of children come to help the crazy gringa.

Leaving Guatemala City after the last field session I spied a few young ceibas waving from the median of the entrance drive to the airport. As I spent my last Guatemalan money before leaving, I decided to keep several of the tiniest coins of all, the five-centavo piece, on which is crammed a miniature image of the giant ceiba.

LIVE OAKS

Live oaks, with their giant, sculpted forms and crazy branches reaching down to the ground, amaze most first-time visitors to the South. To northerners, who have grown up with smaller trees, live oaks have a storybook quality: they fulfill some childhood fantasy of what a tree could be. For several years, a good part of my life was devoted to going "oaking." Fellow graduate students and friends often accompanied me on these adventures through the Louisiana countryside. Tape measure, topographic maps, and camera at the ready, one of us would drive, the other make notes as I called out sightings or pulled to a sudden halt at an interesting specimen. Usually there was a destination; often we didn't get there. Although sharing a common language (more or less) helped, I was a still a foreigner. Once I opened my mouth, they knew I was a Yankee. Fortunately, strangers,

Map 2.2 Research sites and roads traveled in Louisiana

like children, often get the benefit of the doubt and people from all walks of life were patient and helpful (Map. 2.2).

Live Oak Places

Plantation homes with live oak allées, or alleys (double rows of trees or tall shrubs lining walks and drives), were among the first destinations. This icon of the South has been spread far and wide on postcards, book covers, calendars, magazines, travel brochures, and in movies. Joining pilgrims from all over the United States and beyond who come to Oak Alley plantation, I gazed in wonder at the double row of massive trunks, branches arching overhead to create a shady canopy (see Figure 1.2). The allée, which extends behind the house, too, is large enough to show up as a green area on the U.S. Geographic Survey (USGS) topographic map. Although uniform looking from a distance, individual trees vary dramatically in trunk circumference. Strolling up the wide avenue from the mighty river to the richly restored plantation home, I imagined (wrongly) hoop-skirted elegant ladies of 150 years ago, sipping cool drinks in the shade while steamboats plied the waters and the major decision was what to wear that evening.

Like the ruins of Tikal, these plantation homes have been restored to tell a story framed by those living today. Somehow the live oaks, by their shape, size, and obvious age, lend authenticity, a sense of age and rightness to the scene. What is left out in most of the tours, of course, is any mention of slavery, the institution on which all this display of wealth was based. In shops and restaurants, at least in the mid-90s, you could still purchase Mammy dolls. African Americans were conspicuously absent on these tours. Landscapes of white privilege in the past, the plantations seem that way even now. Admission is costly, and the homes are well outside of cities and towns, requiring a car or a riverboat excursion to get there. Gates and fences limit entry. Maintaining the beautiful hushed scene, with manicured lawns, is expensive. Dinner theatres, weddings, and bed-and-breakfast options help many plantations with upkeep.

Houmas House Plantation in Burnside has both an allée and several large individual live oaks. During the house tour, it became obvious that neither the guide nor anyone else in the group was especially interested in live oaks, so I ditched the tour and went looking for Craig Black, the plantation's caretaker, who was rumored to know more about trees.

Craig had been there for fifteen years or more, living with his family in a separate house on the property, next to a single live oak he called Grandmère. Live oaks fascinate him; he called them the "sequoias of the South." The Spanish moss, once so abundant on the live oaks, was wiped out some years ago by a disease, he explained, aided by air pollution from oil refineries. The few trees on the property that sported a good crop of the wispy gray-green strands were there thanks to a movie crew, who had asked permission to "moss" a few trees for authentic background. (Movie crews do all kinds of things to live oaks for filming. For *The Vampire Lestat,* a crew member told me, they wrapped thick layers of padding around the trees to protect both trees and actors when vampires flung themselves through the canopy.)

Craig's most remarkable story, though, concerned the live oak he called Pegleg. It is a very old, lopsided tree. One of its broad branches extends horizontally for a great distance. Craig's daughter likes to have tea there, eight feet above the ground. On the other side of the trunk is what looks like a huge orange growth. Craig put that there, he explained, to cover a wound. A few years ago, the tree suddenly dropped an entire branch. It just missed the group of retired ladies who had been sipping mint juleps in the shade a half hour earlier. Amazed, Craig examined the tree and found it was hollow. After consulting with some tree specialists, he spent days inside the trunk cleaning it out to prevent infection, then covered the hole with wire mesh and a foamy substance that sealed it. If he has his way, this tree will continue to live for a long time. It is still plenty strong. Someone had thoughtfully put a brace under another horizontal branch that appeared to be drooping. During a big storm the brace fell; the branch stayed.[2]

Kathe Hambrick, a fellow graduate student at LSU, added another perception of live oaks in the area. Kathe is African American. She grew up along the Mississippi River, in plantation country. Live oaks, for her, do not evoke nostalgia for a mythical past, but sadness and anger at the long history of slavery. Horizontal live oak branches were often used for hangings, during slavery times and more recently. In spite of her associations, she didn't blame the trees, just as she did not blame today's plantations. Instead, she was busy collecting stories and artifacts for a museum dedicated to African American heritage in the area. Founded in 1994, the River Road African American Museum, located at Tezcuco Plantation, has been a leader in enriching the interpretation of antebellum life, focusing on the experiences and contributions of slaves and their descendants.[3]

Oak plantings at plantations homes vary, from the simple straight allée like the one at Oak Alley, to double rows, long ones up to a mile, curved versions, mixed oak and pine, pairs, single trees or informal groupings, and whole forests of live oaks planted on hills or in front of mansions. Some plantations all the way up to Natchitoches, Louisiana, have live oaks. In spite of all the postcards,

2.11 *Although Afton Villa in St. Francisville burned years ago, its curved allée of live oaks still draws thousands of visitors each year, and its image adorns books, calendars, and postcards.*

though, not all plantations have live oaks. Some feature pecan trees, magnolias, or crape myrtle, or a completely different approach to landscaping. In St. Francisville, in the hills of the Felicianas north of Baton Rouge, is Afton Villa. During the annual springtime "Audubon Pilgrimage," when visitors come to tour the plantations of this area, they are met by women dressed in period costumes. Afton's winding allée, underplanted with bright pink azaleas, is a favorite destination, even though the villa burned a long time ago. During the Civil War, a local story says, Union soldiers riding past didn't bother to plunder this plantation because they thought the allée must lead to a cemetery.

Some of Louisiana's most famous live oaks are single specimens. One of my oaking expeditions was to investigate the Cathedral Oak in Lafayette and the Evangeline Oak in St. Martinville, both listed in the *AAA Guide to Louisiana* as worthy destinations. Driving through narrow streets of a residential neighborhood in Lafayette, hoping to spy some evidence of a huge tree among the houses, I was reminded of walking into Palín on a similar quest.

Church and oak together take up a good part of a block on St. John Street in Lafayette. The cathedral's tall steeple is answered by the oak's long horizontal branches. This is a massive, strong tree that casts dense shade. On that first visit, on a Saturday afternoon, a couple from Texas was also there, drawn by the listing in their AAA guide. Although they had live oaks back home, they said, they'd never seen a tree like this, so massive and old. Some visitors feel free to walk up and touch the tree, or even climb it, while others stay on the paved sidewalk gazing in awe from a (safe) distance. The ground is bare. A low branch in back, just the right height for sitting and swaying, has been worn smooth by hundreds of human bottoms.

During another visit, on a Sunday, I watched from beneath the oak as the procession of priest, attendants, and choir formed at the back of the church. They walked outside to the front entrance, forming a line just visible beneath a low-hanging branch. A choir boy, late, ran clutching billowing robes to keep from tripping. An older man, also gazing at the tree, finally remarked, "Even the squirrel is huge." After Mass, as people gathered for refreshments in front of the church in the hot sun, a longtime parish member told me they used to have coffee under the oak, in the shade. Recent worries that

2.12 *This live oak at St. John's Cathedral in Lafayette is listed as a destination in the AAA guide to Louisiana.*

increased foot traffic was compacting the soil had changed all that. In fact, they were thinking of putting up a fence.

The tree has been there as long as anyone knows—according to the sign nearby it is 450 years old. People of the parish have invested a lot of money to keep it alive and healthy, another fan told me a few weeks later. He had brought an informal tour of friends to admire the tree, and they were busy taking photos while lying on their backs to look up into the canopy. Specialists had been brought in, great sums of money raised, to pay for cabling the major branches to keep the tree in one piece.

The Evangeline Oak

Not far south of Lafayette is St. Martinville, home of the Evangeline Oak. This tree, more than any other single live oak in Louisiana, attracts pilgrims from all over the world. What sets it apart is not size or age or beauty. There are many live oaks along Bayou Teche that would outrank it in any of those categories. Evangeline is honored for its association with the Cajun people, and especially with the heroine of a poem by Henry Wadsworth Longfellow. The story, as told locally by guides and in written materials, is that two lovers, Evangeline and Gabriel, were separated when the French Acadians were expelled from Canada by the British in the eighteenth century. Evangeline searched faithfully for her betrothed, but when she finally found him, under this very live oak on Bayou Teche, he had given up waiting and was married to another. In one version, the young woman lost her mind; in another, she died of a broken heart.

The tree is in a small park on the edge of the bayou. A road off the main drag in the middle of St. Martinville leads right to it. It is surrounded by a simple fence and walkways; an official sign identifies it clearly. Several benches and a small gazebo invite people to linger here. Next door is an old brick building housing a bed-and-breakfast and restaurant. On the other side and across the street conspicuous signs scream about Evangeline mementos. Depending on the time of day and year, this can be a quiet spot to rest or a milling throng of people, some singing and clapping along to live Cajun music. More attractions keep coming. An Acadian museum was being promised in the near future when I was last there in the mid-90s.

Evangeline, like the ceiba at Palín, drew me back for repeated vis-

2.13 The Romero brothers entertain visitors to the Evangeline Oak in St. Martinville with Cajun songs and stories. Photo by Michael Hawkins.

its. Often I'd run into the Romero brothers, who come there whenever tourists are likely, to play music and tell stories. They are local French speakers who took over entertaining at the tree from a previous performer. They'd get a whole group of children sitting around them on the ground, spellbound, while adults stood behind them. Tour buses would cruise by, some slowing for a good view, others allowing passengers to actually get out, take photographs, and shop. Evangeline has been called the most photographed tree in the world. The Romero brothers once showed me the evidence in a glossy French travel book with a two-page spread on them. Once I watched a wedding party being arranged on the gazebo for the official photograph, a fairly common scene there. A shopkeeper brought out a world map with hundreds of pins that showed where people had come from. Many, she said, returned year after year. At Christmas it was too cold for tourists, but the gazebo was decorated with lights.

Images of Evangeline (the oak) decorate town trucks, police cars, signs, and even the arm patch worn by the tiny park's single official ranger. Tours to explain about the tree and the origin of the Cajun people can be arranged in French or English, and with enough warning, the mayor will even meet with groups. Sometimes the guides are dressed in "Evangeline" costumes, clothing presumably worn by Acadians in the late 1700s. The publicity director for the town said they arranged for weddings, and often got requests for the ceremony to be held under the tree. This is not allowed, because the roots must be protected.

Actually, the tree doesn't look healthy. The canopy is sparse, and it got worse over the years I saw it. Examination of the twigs showed it was not growing much. Various explanations were offered. Tour buses idling their engines was causing pollution, said one. Digging up the area around the tree to make the walkways, said another. All the dirt piled on top of the roots during renovations has suffocated them, suggested a third. A virus, according to a fourth. Whatever it is, the tree is sick, perhaps dying. St. Martinville, dependent on this tree for tourists, is worried. When I visited in 1996 the Romero brothers pointed with glee to plastic wrappings on a young branch high in the canopy. "They're cloning the tree," they said. It was an attempt at air-layering begun to start possible replacements should the main tree die. Supposing it succeeded, where would the young trees go? According to town officials, that would be kept quiet. They did not want to risk losing them. Could another tree become the Evangeline tree? Certainly not. This is where Gabriel and Evangeline met, under this tree, I was told firmly.

The waitress in the hotel, where we stopped for tea and pecan pie, said it was the most romantic place in the town, especially on a full moon. Her hope was to have someone, some day, with whom to enjoy it. Had she ever read the Longfellow poem? I asked her. "No," she said, "Guess I should."

I did. One of the booklets billed as a "collectible" contains the whole epic poem plus images of the Evangeline Oak and the statue of Evangeline (the woman) at the nearby Catholic church (the statue is modeled on the actress who played her in a movie). The poem presented a puzzle: nowhere in it is there mention of a live oak (though oaks abound). Even more surprising was that in the poem, the two fictional lovers never met again in Louisiana. Many years after their separation, they saw each other briefly as Gabriel lay dying, an old man, in Philadelphia.

2.14 Stray branches of the Boyd Oak in front of Louisiana's state capitol have been cabled and allowed to snake across the carefully manicured gardens.

Parks

Louisiana does not have plazas like those of Central America, but many towns have a green, a courthouse square, or a park near the center. More often than not, these greens have one or more live oaks. The park in front of the State Capitol in Baton Rouge, for example, has several fine old specimens. Live oaks also front the courthouse and other government buildings. Some courthouse squares are outlined in live oaks. Other towns have live oaks along with a magnolia, a cypress, and crape myrtles. Public parks intended for picnics and celebrations are also home to live oaks. They range in size and age from the ancient grove of live oaks in New Orleans' City Park to smaller and younger plantings all over the state.

Louisianans' favorite activity is celebrating. There are festivals to honor sweet potatoes in Opelousas, sugar in New Iberia, Cajun culture in Lafayette, and shrimp and petroleum in Morgan City. Given the heat most of the year, shade is essential. Lafayette's Festival Acadienne, to celebrate all things Cajun, attracts thousands each year.

Blankets, lawn chairs, picnic baskets, and beer coolers cluster around the live oaks in the park, as people seek the islands of shade while listening to music. Some of the trees there are showing the strain, with exposed roots resulting from compacted soil and subsequent erosion during rainstorms.

Live Oaks as Markers

A trip from Donaldsonville south along Bayou La Fourche revealed other patterns of live oak distribution. Cruising through Donaldsonville, a trusty companion and I spied some good-sized live oaks lining Charles Street. We got out to measure one and found it was almost nine feet in circumference; another was more than ten feet. An older man got out of his pickup truck to find out what was going on. When we asked if he knew anything about the live oaks on the street he said, "I sure do." Old Man Marchant, who was mayor fifty years ago, he told us, had planted them. He remembered that well, because he and some other boys tried to see how far they could bend the young trees and broke off a lot of them. "That's why you don't see so many along here," he said, laughing. The boys were caught and put in jail overnight. "I thought they were some kind of pin oak," he added. Now the trees were a problem, he believed, because the city did not trim them. The tree in front of his sister's house was hitting the roof and filling the gutter with leaves. Another tree in town was growing close to the road. At first they built the road around it, but the roots stuck up so that cars kept hitting it. Finally, the city took it down. Better that way, he thought.

Next stop was the Catholic Church of the Ascension of Our Lord Jesus Christ, which, according to a brochure, was established in 1722, with the present building completed in 1896. Behind the Gothic-style building were four tall live oaks, one of them measuring twelve feet around. Benches placed under the trees were inviting. An old print of the church showed the live oak peeking around from behind, dripping Spanish moss.

We found a similar arrangement later that day farther south in the town of Thibodeaux. St. Joseph Cathedral had six live oaks behind it, along with benches, a fountain, statues, and gravel paths, forming a meditation area. Four more live oaks on the side were covered with ivy and other vines; the trees and a set of statues were sur-

2.15 This is a common scene driving along the Mississippi on River Road—a remnant live oak, once among the largest features in the landscape, dwarfed by industrial plants.

rounded by a fence. The deep shade, with the sounds of water dripping and breeze in the trees, made this a cool, peaceful place.

For a while after Donaldsonville we drove along with the levee on our left, houses on the right. Occasional houses had pairs or rows of live oaks. Then we'd pass an oil refinery, with elaborate pipes crossing the road. Sugarcane fields covered vast stretches of the flat floodplain. Sometimes a single live oak reminded me of the Pacific coast ceibas in their fields—but the oaks were lower, darker, more compact forms that did not wave their arms at the sky.

We stopped at the sight of a lone live oak near a curve of the river, a commanding presence in the landscape in spite of signs of decay. A small house, set back from the road, doors wide open, appeared to belong with the tree. The house was emitting extremely loud music. Persistent knocking on the front door yielded results: an elderly man with deeply tanned skin, dressed in old clothes, emerged. Responding to our question, he told us he was born a few houses down. He figured the live oak was more than a hundred years old, definitely older than he was, because he remembered climbing onto the big limbs when he was a boy. It is, he believes, the "onliest" live oak between here and Oak Alley. When he gives people directions to his house, he says, "The oak will tell you. Can't miss it."

According to local talk, the man told us, some of the tree's branches were shot off during the Civil War. It is completely hollow. Once his son started a fire in it that burned for a week. The telephone company wanted to take off some limbs when they were putting up wires. They decided to take the wood for themselves, until he asked how much they were willing to pay for it. The wires were put on the other side of the road. Before leaving, we asked about measuring the tree and taking some pictures. "I'd like to know how big it is," he said. Twenty-two feet, eight inches in circumference. He waved when I took a photo looking back at his house, a beautiful scene of dark storm clouds behind, deep pink crape myrtle blooming by the green house, and the massive tree in front, as fine a character as the owner.

Continuing along the road, we saw the occasional hulk of a mature live oak, and several rectangular fenced areas with tables and young oaks. These were picnic areas near oil refineries, probably created for employees.

Just as the clouds were lowering and the wind picking up, we spied a whole grove of live oaks, a conspicuous dark area in the mostly open, flat landscape. The trees were old and loaded with moss. St. James Episcopal Church was on the west side of the road; the grove, on the opposite side, marked a cemetery. Nearby we discovered a small historic marker that said the first Acadian settlers in Louisiana arrived here as refugees in 1756–57. Then the storm from the west broke, pouring down rain and blotting out the view. A few miles down the road, we could barely make out the driveways to the St. James school, each lined with a double row of younger live oaks.

Sometimes we saw new homes shaded by much older live oaks. After looking at old travel guides to the area, we realized that these marked former plantation lands now broken up into developments. A motel had been built near one of these old oaks, and named after it. Occasionally we saw trailers, even a trailer park, among such trees, taking advantage of the generous shade they provided.

Most of the Baptist churches along this route did not have live oaks. In fact, these modest, white, one-story buildings tended to be surrounded by extremely neat, trimmed lawns. They were completely different from the gothic Catholic churches we'd seen, with their shady grounds, located within the population centers. Although I began to develop a theory about different attitudes toward physical place and notions of the sacred as shown by landscape styles, I had to scrap this as too general when Baptist churches with magnificent live oaks surfaced later in my travels. Available space, economics, cultural preferences, and social status surely play a role, along with ideas of the sacred.

Cemeteries, too, have different styles. In Donaldsonville, we had seen Bikur Sholem, with cedars lining one side, along with a few crape myrtles and water oaks, and then a Protestant cemetery with just a few sycamores. That was a dramatic contrast with the St. James Episcopal cemetery, and with Catholic cemeteries in that area, which always seemed to have live oaks growing among the above-ground burial sites. Statues, flowers, and other items decorated the graves. A later trip down to the town of Lafitte, south of New Orleans, on All Saints Day (November 1) led to an older style cemetery. Three of us visited this one at night. The cemetery was on a large mound, topped by a live oak. Many of the graves, up and down the mound's slopes, had flickering candles lit for All Saints. Local priests were busy blessing all the cemeteries and relatives of the dead that day.

The Gossip Tree

The Gossip Tree, in the small town of Golden Meadow, would never stop a traveler because of its size or majesty. I found the tree by chance while driving to Grand Isle, trailing a slow school bus one Friday afternoon. Glancing to my right, I noticed a group of men sitting in the shade of a small, scrawny live oak. There hadn't been many oaks along that road, which follows the bayou, so after a moment's hesitation, I pulled over to investigate. As I stood by my car, unsure of a welcome, the group of about nine men gestured to me to come on over. Speaking in strong French accents, they eagerly introduced themselves.

It turned out the tree is famous throughout that part of Louisiana because of this group of men, who meet here every afternoon. They're Cajuns, they explained, and come here to tell stories, catch up on local news, and speak their native French. One man's wife calls it "headquarters," and the local priest refers to them as "the circle of wise men." Their own name for the tree is "La Chêne au Cowan"

2.16 *Live oaks and cemeteries seem to go together. Grace Episcopal cemetery in St. Francisville has a whole forest of live oaks, planted as acorns in the 1800s.*

2.17 *Bigness is not essential to live oak fame. The Gossip Tree in Golden Meadow is famous in the area of Bayou Lafourche for its daily gathering of French-speaking residents.*

(Turtle's oak) after the owner's local nickname. They sit on lawn chairs, swings, and benches. One man, who couldn't speak or walk because of a recent stroke, managed to come over each day on his electric golf cart. They help each other, they said. When someone's wife dies, or leaves, the rest encourage him to go on with life. The tree is a local celebrity—several songs have been written about it.

The live oak was exactly forty-five years old the year I visited, planted the day one of the men got married. In fact, there are two live oaks. The Gossip Tree's trunk features signs documenting the group's history. Each sign has a story, with one including a photograph of Louisiana's former governor, Edwin Edwards. To help keep out the sun, they pick up clumps of Spanish moss along a road farther north, and hang them on the tree. It helps create atmosphere, too. Fishing nets hang from the second oak, waiting to be mended. The picnic table was the site of a crawfish boil when I came back through on Sunday.

2.18 The small cemetery at Chenier Caminada commemorates residents who were swept away by a hurricane because, it is said, they cut down their protective live oaks.

Community Live Oaks

Grand Isle, on the Gulf Coast at the mouth of Barataria Bay, is fond of its oaks for other reasons. The oldest homes on the island, some dating to the 1700s, have survived within a stand of live oaks that protect them from the many hurricanes that sweep through the area. Just west of Grand Isle, a cemetery full of white markers and the remains of one live oak marks the former settlement of Chenier Caminada. In 1893, it was destroyed by a hurricane that swept away all the homes and killed every resident. They cut down their oaks, it is said, instead of protecting them.

Today Grand Isle is a mecca for bird-watchers, who come each spring to see migrants returning from across the Gulf of Mexico. I watched them, wandering around the live oak–lined neighborhoods with binoculars, exclaiming over unusual species and sharing good viewing spots. As the island has become more crowded with fishing camps and other vacation dwellings, some of the oaks have been threatened and islanders are now fierce in their protection of these trees.

The live oaks are not big and stately like those by the plantations. Although gnarled like their larger relations, they are almost scruffy looking, growing lower to the ground, and often lopsided because of the wind and salt spray. In a few places they make shady tunnels along smaller lanes. One native resident-turned-birding-guide explained how island truck farmers, who used to grow some of the earliest vegetables for markets up north, scattered acorns along field margins to create hedgerows and windbreaks.

I stumbled on one legendary Grande Isle live oak by chance. Growing in a fenced backyard among the oldest homes, it was relatively tall. At its base a statue of the Virgin Mary had fresh flowers. The owner, sitting on a swing in the tree's shade with her grandchildren, told me that family traditions here included Mass celebrated under the tree for special occasions. The tree is called the Lafitte Oak. Jean Lafitte was a notorious pirate of the early 1800s. He and his men used Grand Isle as a base for years and many there claim descent from various pirates. Lafitte's name shows up often in the region in connection with buried treasures, burial sites, and specific historic events. One live oak on the island was identified as a sort of post office for secret messages among the pirates.

Other towns in Louisiana are also proud of their live oaks. Hammond, Louisiana, has gone all out. This railroad town east of Baton Rouge held a live oak day in 1995, complete with walking, biking, and driving tours to visit important trees. Frank Neelis, a town resident and leader of the oak lovers, had read about my work in the newspaper. He invited me to come and see their trees, and we spent a day riding around the town viewing live oaks. After Hurricane Andrew, he told me, they realized that far fewer live oaks than other species were damaged by the winds. A grant paid for a complete inventory of damage to trees on private and public lands, during which participants discovered and mapped 155 live oaks, many of them quite old. Many were enrolled in the Live Oak Society, an organization with headquarters right in Hammond that keeps records on hundred-year-old trees.

Among the celebrities we visited were the Peter Hammond Oak, named for the city's founder, who is buried there, along with "his favorite slave boy." The tree forms a small park. Another was the Traveler's Tree, once a resting place at an important cross-roads. Southeastern Louisiana University has many live oaks on its Hammond campus. Among them is the Friendship Oak. A bench encircles its trunk, and long branches snake their way to the ground, forming a generous canopy that is a favorite place to study, eat, socialize, and play.

Many less famous oaks, however, are integral to a local sense of place, because of personal, community, and natural events and memories. Some of the names given to them suggest their varied meanings: Nuptial, Sarah's Joy, My Beloved, Desert Storm, Alte Eiche (old oak), Joyous, Preston. The Imperial Oak, on the outskirts of Hammond, doesn't look like much from the highway leading to town. Acres of gray, shimmering pavement dwarf the huge tree that must once have been a welcome stop for pre-car travelers. Loyal supporters lobbied to save it when the shopping center came in, and now it is its own world. Parents and grandparents stop by after shopping so their children can climb along the low branches, jumping, squealing, holding on to steady adult hands. During one visit, I spotted a still figure, leaning among the drooping limbs. He was a truck driver who had walked by while waiting for his vehicle to be serviced, and found himself spellbound by the tree. For nearly half an hour he stood within the enclosing canopy, unmoving. "I've never seen a tree like this before in my life," he told me.

In the central green in Hammond, by contrast, children climbed carefully on an elaborate wooden structure that had been built around a relatively young oak. Stairs led up to a platform that entirely encircled the tree, allowing people to get close without actually touching roots or branches. Structures like this showed up at several schools later in my travels, and I had the same question as with the structures around ceibas—are they for the tree or the children?

As live oak consciousness developed in town, Frank and others began to tackle the problem of utility crews working in oaks. Through extended conversations, visits from specialists, and neighborhood requests, they brought about a conversion in policy. They demonstrated that live oaks can actually protect wires from damage by reducing wind, and that carefully pruned, balanced trees are far more effective than those that are hacked randomly.

Killing Live Oaks

The major villains identified as enemies of oaks are highway and utility crews. I received this letter after an article on my research appeared in the Baton Rouge newspaper, *The Daily Advocate.*

> Help!
> I was a Live Oak tree who was murdered and dismembered recently by members of the LA Highway Dept. I lived along the side of Highway 16 north of Watson for several hundred years. However, last fall someone decided to do away with me, my parents, brothers, sisters, aunts and uncles. Whoever was responsible for this mass murder needs to be hanged from one of my survivor's limbs.

Highway engineers seem to serve an ideal of perfection that does not include trees. The goal is a straight, clear path, without bends, without obstacles of any sort for cars and trucks whizzing along at ever-increasing speeds. Their work is never done; always there is another bend to straighten, a section to widen, a right-of-way to clear, an obstacle to remove. Pity the trees that stand in the way, and the people who love them. Meanwhile, in towns and cities where traffic is slower, utility crews are blamed for carving and topping any trees even thinking of interfering with the wires, leaving unbalanced, awkward shapes, even among the live oaks.

Killing a live oak in Louisiana is generally risky business, something akin to murder. One day I arrived in St. Francisville to find that two large oaks in front of a bank had been felled. Local residents were livid. One told me she was so mad she was changing banks. "They have an acorn as their logo!" she said. The bank, meanwhile, contended the trees were dying, and replaced them with young trees. Would the townsfolk have reacted this way to having pecans removed? Another woman in that town confessed she wanted to take down a young live oak in her backyard to get more light for her garden, but she was nervous. "Have to do it some night," she said.

Then there was the story of the Mardi Gras Massacre. Some years ago, it was alleged, the Highway Department, after listening to objections from residents about removing some prize live oaks on a corner they felt had to straightened, showed up when everyone was away celebrating on Fat Tuesday to destroy the trees.

Oak People

Louisiana has its share of oak lovers, who have had a major influence on the fate of live oaks. Most of them know each other, so that if you talk to one, you will be led to others. Steele Burden was a name that kept surfacing, and finally I tracked him down at the Louisiana Folklife Museum, which he founded and gave to LSU. That was only one of his gifts. Turns out he planted at least half of the 1,052 live oaks on campus.

Burden was in his nineties when I met him in January of 1995. He was still planting trees. We had several visits, during which he talked about his years as "groundsman" at LSU from 1932 to 1970. There was no landscaping plan when he started; the campus had been built on an open field. He immediately began planting trees that have since transformed the campus into an urban forest. In the early years, he dug up live oaks in the wild, he told me. Later, as nurseries began to offer them, he bought them. Why live oaks? "Because they're the most beautiful thing in the entire South," he said. "If you leave one thing in your life, leave a live oak. It will live to be five hundred years old." His favorite live oak was one on the LSU campus whose branches had reached the ground. "I can't believe I planted it," he said. That tree, near the athletic buildings, was officially dedicated to him in 1994.

Burden is now buried next to a live oak he probably planted on the grounds of the Louisiana Folklife Museum. At a memorial service shortly after his death in 1995, people piled flowers on his grave, then stood in a circle to pray and sing a few hymns. They spoke about how grateful they were for the trees he had planted, and said that they would always think of him in connection with their live oaks.

Arborist Randy Harris inherited responsibility for LSU's live oaks after Burden retired in the early 1990s. For a Yankee (he's from New Hampshire), he is pretty knowledgeable about this Southern tree and as determined to care for them as Burden was to plant them. He fussed over his charges like a parent. When he came to LSU, many of the trees were suffering root compaction, lack of nutrients, general neglect. The problems on campus, he found, are similar to those in many urban situations. "It's so simple," he kept saying about what the trees needed. Instead of fancy soil treatment, fertilizing, spraying, and drastic pruning, he just wanted to add a layer of compost and fence off the trees to keep students from walking on their roots. Over the years, he had worked on refining his methods. He knew each tree intimately, and taught me how to read their condition. Tracing die-back in the canopy, we saw how it related to root problems below. He could tell by the condition of twigs and the shade of green at different times of year how a live oak was doing. He'd pick up a handful of soil from below a tree that had been well mulched for a while and compare its structure and the number of root hairs to those of a tree in the open, not yet treated. He'd point out the difference between the hanging Spanish moss, which did little or no damage to the trees, and the recently increasing ball moss, a pest that eventually restricts light and growth. Many of the campus trees had dead limbs, he said, and he fretted about them falling on people. There was not enough funding to get the work done, and his compost-making project to feed the trees had been discontinued. People took the trees for granted, he said, not realizing they were under stress.

Randy has since moved on to another tree job in the area, and the trees at LSU have found new champions. They've been mulched, and their roots protected in other ways as well. According to Paul Orr, state urban forester, those in charge realized the tremendous role of the trees on campus and decided to put resources into keeping them healthy.

Young Live Oaks

Young live oaks were harder to identify than young ceibas, because they are not nearly as distinctive and they can be confused with other species. Eventually, though, as I learned to pick them out by their characteristic shade of green, texture, and shape, I was astonished by how many had been planted in subdivisions as entrances to shopping malls and private homes. As one nurseryman said, "Everyone wants a live oak, no matter how little room they have."

Growing live oaks for sale in Louisiana is big business. At Live Oak Gardens Wholesale Nursery at Jefferson Island, Joey Billeaud, in charge of growing nursery stock, told me that until recently he was selling one hundred thousand trees per year, all started from acorns. He gets acorns from a row of planted trees that line the

2.19 Joey Billeaud of Live Oak Gardens nursery raises thousands of live oaks each year, patiently shaping them into the preferred "lollipop" form to encourage upright growth.

approach to Live Oak Gardens, preferring to collect from what he considers good-looking trees (though he has no proof that such efforts matter much, given that the flowers are open-pollinated). As the young trees grow he grooms them to a "lollipop" shape—a long single stem up to seven feet tall with a burst of growth at the top. It is a time-consuming task. Landscapers want upright-growing trees that are suitable for street plantings, and for lawns that must be mowed.

Big nurseries like Live Oak Gardens play an important role in the dissemination of live oaks. The trees from Live Oak Gardens are sold all over the South to nurseries who eventually sell them to homeowners. Thousands of the trees used to go to Florida, where they seemed to believe Louisiana live oaks were superior to the local trees. They still ship to Texas. Genetic stock from this particular group of trees is thus achieving a wide distribution. In some years, when there has not been a good crop, they have obtained seed from a nursery in Alexandria.

The shape and condition of live oaks can tell a lot about the people who own them. Those with the sculpted clean lines and branches high enough to clear the lawn and arch gracefully over the house belong in upper-class neighborhoods. They often have lights mounted strategically to show off their form at night. I met more than one homeowner who felt guilty and embarrassed at the condition of their trees if they did not meet this ideal. It costs a small fortune to maintain them that way, because they must be pruned periodically to keep from getting "messy." Specialists in tree care, with costly equipment to reach into the canopy, abound in the yellow pages. While some insist the trees must be kept pruned for health, others are equally sure the trees know what they are doing, and the degree of pruning is a style issue. Arborist Randy Harris has nothing but scorn for those heavily pruned trees. If live oaks grow leaves within the canopy, he explained, it's because they need them. During the heat of summer, evergreen trees like the live oak shut down photosynthesis in the outer canopy. In the dimmer light within, where it is also cooler, leaves can continue to function, providing important nutrients, especially for trees under stress. The "natural" approach was gaining adherents when I was interviewing people in the mid-90s

PATTERNS AND QUESTIONS

While sorting through slides of live oaks and ceibas after a few years, I was startled to find that they began to form pairs. Different as they were, the two species showed up in similar landscape situations. Both were the tree of choice for official government buildings, churches, schools, and other culturally important sites. However, a single ceiba was sufficient to mark many of these places, while live oaks often showed up as formal or informal group plantings.

Both trees were often distinguished from ordinary species by having special surrounding structures, like fences and raised planters. These varied dramatically in style, however. In Guatemala they were likely made of cement, while Louisianans preferred wooden surrounds and rope fences. The approach was less formal, softer. Signs, too marked both species, helping to explain the significance of the tree. In Louisiana, however, signs more often announced a historic association, connected to this particular tree or place, and often gave a specific name for the tree. In Guatemala, the ceiba was identified as the national tree, and the person or persons responsible for the structures around it were named.

Ceibas were more likely to have painted trunks, something only occasionally observed among live oaks. When asked about why ceibas are painted, Guatemalans most often told me it was to keep harmful insects from crawling up the tree. Some just shrugged. Along roads, they told me, the white color reflects light, warning drivers who might be aiming for the trunk. During one bus ride, my seat companion, who had been filling me in on ceiba stories, pointed out that the red and blue colors on a ceiba we passed represented a political party. So there are many potential messages embodied in this practice.

Names are another important difference. Those for the live oak are personal, historic, locational, or indicate some state of being. They suggest a relationship that can be familiar and intimate. Ceiba names, if a tree has one beyond being called the *árbol nacional*, are strictly associated with a place—Palín, Palencia, Colonia Hunapú.

Care for the trees is also dramatically different. In Louisiana a whole class of experts exists to propagate, plant, and prune the trees, and there are distinct styles and even arguments about how to do this right. Not once did I hear anything of the sort about ceibas, except for concern that a tree had been damaged by vandals. The trees seem to be on their own. Yet ceibas did present a puzzle about their growth form. Why did ceibas in the wild tend to be tall, while those in plazas were almost always broad and spreading?

Ceibas and live oaks dominate many spaces where people gather for various reasons—markets, festivals, religious celebrations, relaxation, eating. Social interaction is thus influenced in some way by their placement in the landscape, and by their ability to shape human experience of place. Shade is one reason—both the study areas can be extremely hot.

A major difference is that live oaks are far more common at private homes than are ceibas. The ceiba is a more public, formal sort of tree, while the live oak is able to be both public and private. Yet family pride can be associated with both: planters of ceibas are often commemorated on signs or by their family. Live oaks are more likely to be named after a family member or to mark the family home.

Children interact differently with these two trees. Both provide

2.20 *The moss-draped oaks of City Park are sacred to some. This student reported she had asked the trees for help — and found inspiration for a creative writing project.*

private spaces among the roots and something to walk around and hide behind. Once they are large trees, though, the ceibas are hard to get up into. Thorns on the trunk and branches are discouraging, and since the trees tend to drop lower limbs and grow very fat smooth trunks, most interactions have to happen while children stand on the ground. Live oaks, on the other hand, are everyone's fantasy of a climbing tree, especially ones allowed to grow so their limbs touch the ground. People throughout the South have added swings, easily placed on the long horizontal limbs, and all manner of ladders and tree houses that encourage being in among the branches. Some people told me of actually running through the limbs of live oaks at their school when they were young, something they suspected would not be allowed now for fear of accidents. Yet while live oaks are more inviting, ceibas more aloof, they both attract children.

These observations suggested some questions regarding the role of these trees as sacred, and the very idea of what sacred means in different cultural contexts. The ceiba is clearly a sacred tree in the sense of being set apart from the ordinary—at least many of the trees were. But individuals within the species were not necessarily accorded respect. In terms of being the site of religious or other sacred events, I witnessed few, although people did speak of festivals held beneath ceibas and hinted at ritual activities in some lowland areas. On the other hand, live oaks, although seldom referred to as sacred, and having no official status as a state tree, were more consistently treated as special. They also played starring roles in weddings, funerals, Masses, and private meditations. Once I found a young woman under one of the oldest oaks in City Park, New Orleans, who had written a prayer to the "moss tree," as she called it, asking for help with the screenplay she was writing for school.

Encounters with ceibas and live oaks in their landscapes showed the variety of ways they engage with people. Clearly, this was far more complex than I had at first thought, with variations at the individual, local, and regional level. Individual trees can have particular shapes and characters important to their immediate community, yet invisible to outsiders. Attitudes toward each species also varied, within and across cultural groups. The question of why these two trees had been singled out was not yet clear. But what if we consider the trees as active agents? Each tree species has particular ways of growing and responding to life in human-managed environments. What was it about the trees themselves that might fit them for life with people? Clues emerged as I pieced together their natural history.

Chapter 3

NATURAL HISTORY

THE SECRET LIVES OF CEIBAS AND LIVE OAKS

TREES, LIKE HUMANS, are astonishing in their diversity. Each species has a finely developed set of strategies to help it grow and reproduce. There are trees with long, flexible trunks that sway in the slightest breeze, leaves forming delicate traceries; hulking monsters with tough, thick, leathery leaves that hang on to moisture; tiny alpine willows only a few inches tall at maturity; and aggressive strangler figs that smother their hosts from the top down. Some drop their leaves part of each year, then expend a lot of energy to produce the next flush; others hang on to them for years at a stretch. Their flowers range from the inconspicuous to the flamboyant, and propagules from bits of branches or creeping roots to dust-like seeds and fruits that can weigh more than a hundred pounds. Success depends on each tree's adaptability to surrounding conditions, including soils, climate, and a host of other organisms who nibble on them, pollinate their flowers, distribute their seeds, and sometimes manage to invade their tissues. Humans are among these others.

Life with humans is a mixed blessing for trees. People have singled out some as worthy of saving, others as dispensable. Ceibas and live oaks have succeeded for the time being in finding a home within the human-controlled landscapes in much of Guatemala and Louisiana. Part of this is the result of deliberate human decisions. On the other hand, considering the situation from the trees' point of view, these two species have some adaptations that predispose them for human-controlled environments. In fact, they sometimes benefit unexpectedly from the relationship.

CEIBA, *Ceiba pentandra*

The ceiba belongs to the tropical family *Bombacaceae*. Fat, swollen trunks are frequent in this family as a way to store water in dry areas. One cousin, the giant baobab of Africa, can measure up to 148 feet in girth. The family includes several other notable species among its approximately 31 genera and about 225 species: the durian of Asia, known for its smelly but delicious fruit; balsa, which produces the lightest and softest of woods; and the red silk cotton tree of India, which bears spectacular red flowers long used in sacred rituals.

Botanists have at various times despaired of ever creating order in this family. Young trees of different species and even genera look very much alike. They flower irregularly, and are highly variable, leading to many misidentified specimens. Their distribution is no easier to understand. People have carried trees, seeds, and fruits around the world with them for eons, making their original distribution difficult to establish. The baobab, native in Africa, Madagascar, and northwestern Australia (presumably reflecting the results of continental drift), can now be found growing happily in Hawaii and Florida.

Ceiba pentandra appears to be equally at home in the Americas, Africa, and Asia, a highly unusual situation. Members of the same genus often inhabit both hemispheres, but are usually represented by separate species. Geographers and botanists have wondered about this situation for years; some thought the ceiba might support the notion of pre-Columbian contacts between Africa and the Americas.

Herbert Baker, a botanist, spent years studying the various ceibas of Africa to try to resolve some of the confusion. On that continent, and in Asia, the ceiba is a commercial tree, grown in plantations. The silky fibers produced in its pods are good for stuffing, insulation, and life jackets. Baker didn't think the ceiba was native to Asia, nor did he hold with the pre-Columbian contact theory. After floating pods in salt water for weeks and testing to see if seeds could still germinate, he concluded the ceiba *could have* traveled from the Americas to Africa on its own. However, patterns of diversity and disease resistance proved to him that ceibas were native to both America and Africa. He further suggested that a cultivated form of the ceiba, selected in Africa, was introduced to Southeast Asia for kapok production. *Ceiba pentandra* was probably in Java as early as the tenth

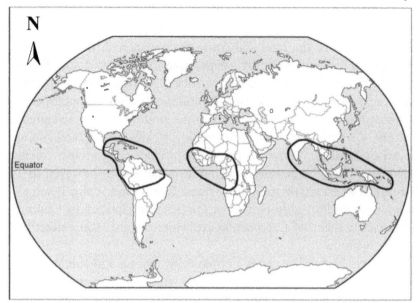

Map 3.1 Global distribution of Ceiba pentandra. *Map adapted from Baker 1965.*

century and has since managed to spread outside of cultivation, so regularly that it passes as a native. Unless someone reopens the investigation, *C. pentandra* is presumed native to the American tropics and western Africa.[1]

Taxonomy

The word "ceiba," used as both scientific and common name today, is probably from an Arawak word for canoe used by the indigenous people of the Caribbean Islands. They made canoes out of whole trunks (and still do in Jamaica). The Spanish adopted that name for the tree and brought it to the mainland; many places throughout the region still bear the name ceiba or variations on it, like ceibo, ceibilla, ceibito, and ceibal.[2]

At least two species of the genus *Ceiba* grow in Guatemala: *Ceiba pentandra* (L.) Gaertn. and *C. aesculifolia* (H.B.K.) Britt. & Baker.[3] They often grow in the same area, and to the uninitiated look very much alike. The best way to tell them apart is by their flowers. Flowers of *C. aesculifolia* are much larger, 10–16 cm (3.9–4.7 in.) long. Unfortunately, flowers are present only briefly each year (if at all), which makes this a tough characteristic to use for identification. Those who work the land and come in contact with the two trees regularly tell them apart by shape, size, and bark color. Some describe *C. aesculifolia* as much more prickly. According to Paul Standley and Julian Steyermark, two intrepid botanists who published a series of floras of Central America in the first half of the twentieth century, *C. aesculifolia* has more conic prickles that cover young branches, while *C. pentandra* has short prickles and smooth young branches. This characteristic is highly variable too, however, as I found out when trying to identify trees. Even flower color is sometimes in question; although most species descriptions in Central America say those of *C. pentandra* are white or pink, some describe them as yellow.[4]

Growth form also varies dramatically among individual trees. Some have widely spreading branches, while others are quite tall; some show a regular branching pattern, while others are highly contorted. In his study of African ceibas, Herbert Baker identified three distinctively shaped varieties of *Ceiba pentandra*. A tall upright form he called the American and African Spiny. The second form, called African Spineless, is typical of the savannas. It is much shorter, only to about 15.25 m (50 ft.) tall, forms no buttresses and spines, and has thicker bark. Branches ascend instead of reaching out at right angles, and the main trunk often forks. The third type he believes to be a naturally occurring hybrid between the first two, selected by people for several advantages: trees are moderate in height, have easily climbable branches, are spineless, and produce annual fruits that remain on the tree when ripe, making harvest easy. Baker notes this form only occurs where it has been planted, so he calls it the "African cultivated form." It is propagated by cuttings only and commonly grows at entrances to villages, along roads, in groves, and on plantations. This African cultivated form is also the ceiba of Southeast Asian kapok plantations.

No similar study has been conducted for American ceibas. Some writers have described a distinctive strain of Caribbean ceiba called *C. caribaea* (DC.) A. Chev. or *C. pentandra* var. *caribaea* (DC.) Bakh. It has a shortened trunk and many buttresses. Marshall Howe, writing in 1906, found both this form and the tall kind on the islands, but only the tall form on the mainland. The shorter ceibas may be the result of severe and recurring damage from hurricanes, but there

3.1 Visitors to Tikal pass by this exemplary ceiba, showing off buttresses ten feet tall and a straight, columnar trunk, topped with spreading branches that suggest why it was imagined as holding up the sky.

might well be several distinct varieties or subspecies, as there are in Africa. A thorough taxonomic study of the group is long overdue.

During fieldwork, I found that people in Guatemala have differing notions about the category ceiba. Most often, the ceibas pointed out to me were the type that taxonomists refer to as *C. pentandra*, but occasionally they were not. Most were at least closely related trees, like the other ceiba species (*C. aesculifolia*) or a member of the genus *Bombax*. Occasionally, though, any large tree could be called ceiba. There were also some ceibas called *machos* (males) or *hembras* (females), an interesting distinction since ceibas are all self-fertile trees. The terms may refer to some other distinctive characteristic, although I was unable to determine what that might be. Since the main questions of this study dealt with human-tree relationships, I recorded what people said about what they called "ceibas" and did my best to verify the identity of the tree in question.

Distribution and Ecology

On the basis of where ceibas can be found today, it would be easy to conclude that their natural distribution is throughout Central America, except perhaps in the coldest highlands. According to Standley and Steyermark's *Flora of Guatemala*, however, *Ceiba pentandra* is native only to moist or dry plains and hills below 1,000 m (3,281 ft.). That roughly delimits the *tierra caliente*, or warm tropical zone. The other species, *C. aesculifolia*, reaches up to 1,500 m (4,921 ft.). These boundaries are approximate; microclimates vary, so individual trees have probably long managed to survive a bit higher. What limits the trees to this area? One possibility is minimum temperature during pollination and fruit set. Herbert Baker found that in Africa, fruit would not set if temperatures fell below 20° C (68° F) at this crucial time. Whatever the reason, the trees apparently do not produce pods in the higher areas. If planted, though, they grow, even thrive, at higher elevations for many years.[5]

Ceibas were among the first trees noted by the Spanish explorers in 1494 on the island of Española, where they described trees bearing "wool."[6] Today they are still common throughout the Caribbean Islands and in the tropical forests of Mexico and Central America. They are cultivated as far north as the deserts of Hermosillo in Mexico, as well as in Florida and California. In South America, ceibas inhabit tropical lowland forests all the way to the southern Amazon basin.

On a local scale, tracking the ceiba's native range is more complex. Like the other countries of Middle America, Guatemala contains an amazing variety of habitats among its tall mountains, lush valleys, and extensive coastal and inland plains. Ceibas play different roles within these different habitats. In the northern lowlands of the Petén, in the tierra caliente, ceiba is a regular component of the native tropical rainforests that cover this large area of rolling low hills, mostly less than 600 m (1,968 ft.) above sea level. At about Flores, the northern seasonal dry forest becomes the hot and humid southern evergreen forest, with little seasonal variation in temperature.

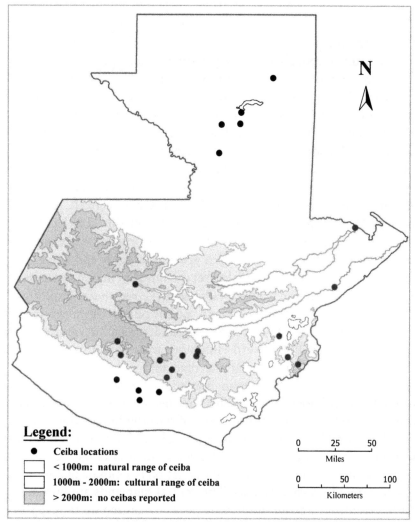

Map 3.2 *Natural and cultural distribution of ceiba in Guatemala.*

Directly to the south of the Petén rises the Alta Verapaz mountain range. This region of cool, moist forests is home to the resplen-
dent quetzal, the national bird of Guatemala, and the orchid monja
blanca, the national flower. Ceibas also grow within the region, but
are not a dominant feature of these forests.

Flowing out of this region to the east is the Río Polochic. Karl
Sapper, a German who traveled up this river in the 1880s, noted
giant ceibas bordering both sides as the river ascended into the Alta

Verapaz.[7] Ceibas are also prominent around low-lying Lake Izabal. The lower Motagua River, where it approaches the Caribbean coast, is ceiba country, too. Near the Mayan ruins at Quiriguá, several large ceibas grow amid the tropical rainforest vegetation that stretches to the coast. The upper valley to the west becomes hotter and drier, eventually forming a pocket of true desert and savanna that pushes into the center of the country, almost to the capital. Both *Ceiba pentandra* and *C. aesculifolia* grow in this region, along the river and the dusty highway, and sometimes in fields.

South of the Motagua valley lies the Oriente, a region of low mountains and hills, seasonally dry. Both species of ceiba (*C. pentandra* and *C. aesculifolia*) also grow here. Much of this area has been cleared, grazed, and planted, so little of the original vegetation is intact. Many stocky ceiba-like trees grow in pastures and along the road, most probably *C. aesculifolia*. Yet the bus stop in one town near Esquipulas was located under a tall, classic *C. pentandra*. Exploring the land around Esquipulas, I found several ceibas within the town that had been planted (by a resident's grandfather), but on the outskirts of town, heading toward Honduras, were young trees in pastures and disturbed areas near the road that were clearly spontaneous. Just over the Honduran border to the south lies Copán, where the well-known Mayan ruins have been invaded by enormous contorted ceibas that grow atop some of the crumbling pyramids.

The central highlands of Guatemala, the most densely populated section of the country, lie above the ceiba's natural range. At elevations of a mile or more, the natural vegetation is a mosaic of pine and oak forest and grassy savannas. The central highlands are bordered on the south by a chain of volcanic peaks that reach up to 4,267 m (14,000 ft.). They form a northwest-southeast line parallel to the coast, the beginning of Central America's volcanic spine. Descending rapidly to the Pacific coast is the area known as La Costa, its upper reaches once covered with lush evergreen rainforest, the lower forest and grass-covered plains stretching to the Pacific Ocean. This region, too, has long been altered by humans, who have replaced the natural vegetation with a succession of crops including cacao, coffee, sugar, and cotton.

My observations during several trips through the gradient to the Pacific coast tend to confirm Standley's statement that ceibas are native to areas below about 1,000 m (3,281 ft.). Just below Palín, elevation 1,135 m (3,724 ft.), the road dips into ceiba country. Above this, the only ceibas I noted were in cultivation, the one exception being a large single tree by the road between Palín and Amatitlán (which may have been planted long ago). Below Palín, ceibas begin to show up in pastures. Two other transects along roadways down that gradient, the first from Antigua, Guatemala, to El Rodeo, the second from Lake Atitlán to Cocales Junction, suggest the limit is between 1,000 and 1,200 m (3,281 and 3,937 ft.).

Along the Pacific coastal highway between Escuintla and Cocales many large old ceibas stand out in pastures, in sugarcane fields, and along the road. Edgar Geovany Mendoza, a Guatemalan ethno-botanist, told me that older residents of the area say there were once many more ceibas that measured up to 4 m (13 ft.) in diameter (more than 40 ft. in circumference). They were part of the vast forests that covered the coastal plains before the road was put through. Conversations with Guatemalans who live or travel in that region confirmed that large ceibas are characteristic of the Pacific coastal area; some patches of forests with many large ceibas are said to survive along the southeast coast between San José and El Salvador.

Cultural Distribution

In their 1949 *Flora of Guatemala*, Standley and Steyermark remarked that ceibas had long been planted above their natural range. My fieldwork confirmed that this is still true today. Map 3.2 shows dots of ceibas in cultural contexts I either saw or have reliable information about. Many are between 1,000 and 1,500 m (4,921 ft.), but some are closer to 2,000 m (6,562 ft.). The area between 1,000 and 2,000 m (3,281 and 6,562 ft.) is therefore designated as the ceiba's cultural distribution, the area in which the trees exist because people have planted them (see Map 3.2).

One thing to keep in mind is that in much of Guatemala one need not travel great distances to find a ceiba to transplant. The land is so steeply dissected that pockets of tierra caliente, the ceibas' home, snake their way well inland from the coastal lowlands. The two large ceibas in Los Mixcos, for instance, have lowlands nearby. Anyone determined to plant a ceiba can also take a bus to the coast and get one for little or nothing by digging up a wild-grown tree or visiting a nursery.

Life Cycle

Ceibas start out life as small, round, oily, protein-rich brown seeds. They are packed in masses of silky fibers in a durable pod. When the pods ripen they split, and the fibers, measuring up to 3 cm (1.2 in.) long, expand into fluffy white or tan clouds that carry the seeds on the wind. Some pods fall to the ground unopened, the seeds nestled safely inside, protected from excessive heat and water by the fibers. If they fall into a stream or other body of water, they can last for months. Washed up on shore, they open and release unharmed seeds. Trees can also start from cuttings. In Southeast Asia, where ceiba is grown in plantations for kapok production, this is an important form of propagation, and the only way to be sure of reproducing a particular strain. Cuttings of young shoots are planted right out in the field.[8]

Ceibas are opportunists. Although they can be part of mature forests, they come in during early stages, when things are not settled. They are colonizers of disturbed habitat, quickly taking advantage of

3.2 Leaves and pod of ceiba. The silky fibers eventually fluff and spill out, carrying seeds off in the slightest breeze.

open, sunny spots and of light gaps in the forest created when other species fall. Unlike many such colonizers, though, they persist for a long time, remaining as part of mature forests. In the wild, these habitats are common on the edges of streams and other bodies of water, locations where ceibas are often found in great numbers. This pioneer quality means the ceiba is predisposed to do well when people clear forests for agriculture or roads. The Pacific lowlands, for instance, have long been an important agricultural area, so the relationship between people and ceibas is likely a long one.[9]

Seeds that find a suitable open, well-watered habitat grow rapidly. In the Pacific lowlands around Siquinala, where mature trees distribute abundant seed, the owner of a nursery explained that ceibas spring up all over the place during the rainy season, from May to October, and grow to 2.5 m (8 ft.) or more by the following February. Ceibas tolerate a wide range of soils, from sandy to clay. Spines protect them from grazing or rubbing animals. They wear off the trunk as the trees age, though newer branches may continue to be prickly. Branches arise in regular whorls of three, one per year. They or the scars of dropped branches are visible on mature trees unless the growth tip is damaged, when a more contorted form develops. Buttresses begin to develop early, extending toward the prevailing wind. They act like cables, helping to anchor the tree.

By age three to four, the trees start to flower. In its flowering strategy, ceiba differs from other members of the family Bombacaceae. Most open a few flowers at a time over a long period. Ceiba, by contrast, flowers in one major burst when the tree is leafless, generally at the beginning of the rainy season. Compact ball-shaped clusters (fascicles formed by shortened internodes) sprout on horizontal branches. Often only part of the tree flowers. The first time I visited the ceiba of Palín, a few branches were covered with flowers while the rest were bare. The pink or white flowers are fleshy and thick, typical of bat-pollinated blooms. They open about 6:30 in the evening, and by the next afternoon fall off.

The blossoms, which produce abundant nectar and pollen, are an important food source for a variety of animals. Victor Manuel Toledo, in a study of rainforest pollination in Veracruz, Mexico, observed the following visitors to ceiba blossoms: several species of bats, seven species of hummingbirds, plus twenty-six other species of birds, bees, wasps, small beetles, opossum, and squirrels. Bats are important pollinators in all regions where the ceiba grows; in Samoa, the flying fox is its only pollinator. Even the spent blossoms are valued by wildlife—cattle eat them when they fall to the ground.[10]

Botanists who tracked ceiba flowering patterns found that the timing and frequency varies dramatically. In Samoa, for instance, the trees flower every year, while in the forests of Barro Colorado Island in Panama, ten years can go by between flowering episodes. For Herbert Baker, the consistent annual flowering of African cultivated ceibas confirmed his notion that these were strains deliberately selected from the wild for kapok production. Like flowering, fruit set seems to be more consistent in open settings than in the forest. Ceibas in kapok plantations reliably yield six hundred pods per year, and Herbert Baker counted four thousand fruits on a single tree.

Ceibas are resilient, adaptable trees, and highly variable in form. In favorable situations with plenty of water, light, and warmth, they continue to grow rapidly for years. Sometimes they reach a height of 12 m (40 ft.) in three years. Like many tree species, ceibas have a central growth point, a dominant shoot that continues to grow upward while the branches spread horizontally. In a forest situation, they gradually shed the lower branches through a natural pruning process. A ceiba whose central leader is damaged can develop a very different shape. Sometimes a new central leader emerges, but often growth is diverted in a more horizontal direction. In Los Mixcos, a village in the hills above Guatemala City, there are two ceibas, both planted during the 1800s in an open field in the middle of town. One tree has grown straight and tall, while the other, of equal girth, is much shorter and broader. As mentioned earlier, it is possible there are several genetic strains, but in this case, as for many trees growing in the open, I believe damage to the growth point is a more likely reason. Lightning, wind, disease, and human interference are all possible causes. The important factor, in terms of understanding human-tree relations, is that ceibas are quick to respond to damage by regrowing branches; they are able to assume a number of shapes to continue growth for many years.

Ceiba wood is so soft and coarse that it has little commercial value. It is pinkish-white to ashy-brown, and has no taste or odor. When first cut, it can be wet and heavy, but it dries to a weight of 27 lb. (12.3 kg) per cubic foot and tends to discolor or rot. In the Caribbean Islands, whole trunks were, and still are, carved to make canoes. When I asked about this in the Petén lowlands, boatmen laughed at the idea because the wood is too soft to last. They make canoes out of *caoba* (*Swietenia*), they told me. Botanical descriptions often list a range of objects that can be made from the soft wood, including boxes and matches, and in 1939 logs were shipped from Guatemala to Germany for making plywood. A few residents of the Pacific coast said people sometimes use it for subflooring when building homes, even though cutting the trees is illegal.[11]

Legend has it that the ceiba of Palín is 450 years old. Most botanists believe the species' life span is more like two to three hundred years. The problem is, there is no reliable way to determine the age of a ceiba other than by finding out when it was planted. Taking cores is not helpful: the wood is so open, and the growth so nearly continuous, that there are no distinct rings to count; the heartwood blends into the sapwood. A hundred-year-old individual can be enormous, suggesting it must be ancient. The Palín tree, the largest one I measured, was 10 m (33 ft.) in circumference.

At the time of the conquest, six hundred years after the end of the Maya classic period (A.D. 300–900), huge ceibas, far larger than the largest trees in plazas today, reportedly existed in Central America. Oviedo y Valdez, who traveled throughout the area in the 1520s, said Nicaragua had the biggest ceibas.

I shall speak only of a ceyba which I saw many times, less than half a league from the residence of the Cacique of Guacama, which belongs to the grant of a man called Miguel Lucas, or his companions Francisco Núñez and Louis Farfán. This tree I measured with my own hands by a cabuya cord, and found its circumference at the base to be 33 varas, or 132 spans [88 feet]; and since it stood on the bank of a river it was not possible to measure the lowest portion of the roots; if properly measured, I judge its circumference would have been 36 varas or 144 spans [96 feet].[12]

I tried to date some of the historic trees of Guatemalan plazas to see if there were clues about their life span. Several of the ceibas famous for their size and age in Guatemala in the 1960s have since died, including those at Amatitlán, Escuintla, and Palencia. What little I found seems to corroborate the two- to three-hundred-year life span. The tree of San Francisco Petén (Figures 2.10 and 5.1) was

3.3 Oropendulas, colony-nesting birds of the rainforest, have suspended their hanging nests from the spreading branches of this well-known ceiba on the road to Tikal. Photo by William V. Davidson.

planted in 1828, according to a town history, and appears to be in good health.

Older trees become entire ecosystems. The massive, horizontal branches are convenient homes for a vast array of epiphytes, plants that perch atop other species to reach light. Often ceiba branches are completely covered with bromeliads, many kinds of orchids, ficus species, philodendron, pepperomium, anthocereus (a cactus), ferns, mosses, and lichens.[13] Densely packed on the layered branches, these assemblies form a distinct upper-level ecosystem. One such tree can thus be a major contributor to the biodiversity of an area, whether forest or town.

LIVE OAK, *Quercus virginiana*

The Southern live oak, *Quercus virginiana*, is part of a genus that has been of central importance to humans through much of the temperate regions. Oaks used to dominate the old forests in large areas of Europe, Asia, and North America. They have offered people acorns, timber, even cork for wine bottles. Other members of the family Fagaceae, distributed throughout the world's temperate and tropical regions except in Africa, include *Castanea* (the chestnuts of Europe, North America, and Japan) and *Fagus* (the beeches).

Botanists have long tried to organize the more than five hundred species of *Quercus* into smaller, more manageable groupings. One familiar division is between white oaks and red oaks. White oaks have more rounded leaf lobes and harder wood. Their acorns mature during the first year and contain fewer tannins, making them sweet to taste. Red oak leaves have sharper points, their wood is softer, and their acorns mature in two years. In order to be edible, they require extensive leaching. Even squirrels prefer the white oak acorns.

Another common division, that between deciduous and evergreen oaks, refers to growth habit. This one cuts across taxonomic groupings. "Evergreen" oak species occur in Europe, Asia, and western and southern North America. In spite of their name, these trees are not true evergreens. They are called evergreen because they stay green year-round, dropping old leaves as the new ones appear (true evergreens keep their leaves for more than one year). *Quercus virginiana* is one of these so-called evergreen oaks. Its leaves do not resemble those of either the white or red oak group described above.

Instead, they are small, leathery, and mostly entire, though some have a bit of lobing near the tips. Common names like "live oak" and "*chêne vert*" (green oak) recognize its ability to remain green. California's live oaks, among them the coast live oak (*Q. agrifolia*) and the interior live oak (*Q. wislizenii*), are a taxonomically separate group from that of the Southern live oak.

Taxonomy

Louisiana's live oaks are part of a *Quercus* subgroup called series *Virentes*, native to the southern United States, Mexico, Central America, and northwestern Cuba. The whole series belongs within the white oaks group. According to a major botanical study done in 1984, there are five species in the series besides *Q. virginiana*. Most are small, shrubby trees that grow on the sandy coast. People often mistake them for stunted Southern live oaks, stressed by the poor soils and lack of water.[14]

A mature live oak growing in the open develops a low, rounded crown up to 120 feet tall, but with a spread of 150 feet or more. Trunks with diameters of 10 feet are not uncommon in older trees. The small leaves, 2 to 5 inches long and ½ to 2½ inches wide, are dark green and glossy on top, while the underside is generally lighter and often pubescent. They stay on the tree through the winter. When new leaves begin to grow in spring the old ones turn brown or yellow and fall. The small flowers are imperfect, born on separate catkins on the same tree. Male flowers shed copious amounts of pollen in spring, covering sidewalks and streets in fine yellow dust. The small acorns grow singly or in pairs. When ripe they measure 15–22 mm (.5–.8 in.) long and 8–15 mm (.3–.5 in.) wide, are dark brown to almost black, barrel shaped, and pointed. About a third of their length is covered by the cap.

One of the ongoing controversies about live oaks is whether the Texas live oak is the same species as the Southern live oak. Texas live oaks are generally smaller, grow in clumps with a number of trunks connected through a single root system, and have a grayer bark. Some consider the Texas tree a subspecies of *Q. virginiana*, while others put it in a separate species, *Q. fusiformis*, with a natural range west of the Brazos River. Nixon concluded there are two separate species. He found they overlap in a roughly triangular area of Texas

3.4 The Back Brusly Oak, longtime community center and cross-roads marker, is host to many other species, including resurrection fern and a crop of Spanish moss.

and Louisiana. A hybrid between the two, which he called *Q. fusiformis* × *Q. virginiana*, ranges from southeastern Texas near Columbus, west to the Edwards Plateau near Austin, and south to Corpus Christi. This matter is far from settled, however, and the older classifications continue to be used.

From time to time people have identified distinct varieties of live oak that may or may not have a genetic base. The sweetness and size of acorns is said to vary, and one source referred to an oil made from some trees that was comparable to olive oil.[15] Growth form is another distinguishing characteristic. Jim Foret, a lifelong forester in Lafayette, has been spotting trees with a naturally upright growth form for propagating as street trees. In southwestern Louisiana two folk categories are the English and Spanish live oaks, the latter being a more upright stocky form than the open and graceful English oaks. Finally, Neil Odenwald, a landscape architect and professor at Louisiana State University, said that he and others believe the degree to which the trees retain their leaves in winter is genetically determined. They choose young trees carefully for landscape planting.

Distribution and Ecology

The live oak's native range extends in a band along the Gulf Coast from the Louisiana-Texas border in the west through the Florida peninsula and up the Atlantic coastal plain as far north as Virginia. The northernmost stand of native oaks was reported from Fort Monroe military base in Virginia in 1935.

Live oaks are dominant forest species in only a limited area, mainly in scattered stands in northern Florida, the Gulf Coast, and the Atlantic coastal plain. This is a region where conditions are highly unstable: hurricanes, fires, droughts, floods, and incursions of saltwater are all common. The result is constantly changing plant communities, a mix of tropical and temperate, evergreen and deciduous species. To survive to maturity, plants must be highly adaptable and persistent. Live oak is such a species. It can grow in a range of soils—sandy, clay, and alluvial—and even tolerates having its roots covered with saltwater at high tide. It is a fast grower and has a low center of gravity. In fact, it seems to have been designed to withstand hurricanes. Its wood fibers are exceptionally strong, and its branches, even

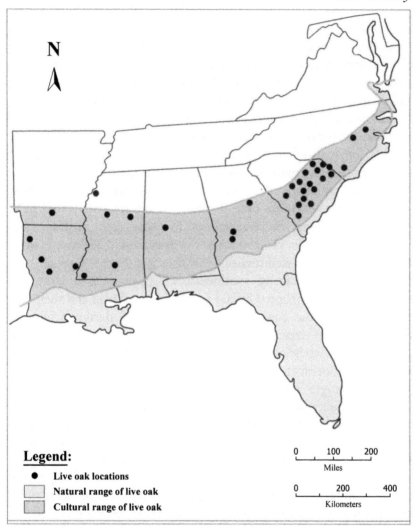

Legend:

● Live oak locations

Natural range of live oak

Cultural range of live oak

| 0 | 100 | 200 |

Miles

| 0 | 200 | 400 |

Kilometers

Map 3.3 Natural and cultural distribution of live oaks in southeastern North America

large ones, amazingly pliable. The leaves also tolerate salt spray, giving it an advantage over many other species.

Distribution maps 3.3 and 3.4 suggest that live oaks grow evenly throughout the southern coastal region, but this is not exactly true. In much of the region, habitats suitable for live oak, and its frequent tropical companion the sabal palm, are only small areas of raised land within larger swampy expanses. In Florida, these are known as hammocks. In the distant past, when the climate was warmer, these plant communities were probably more widespread. Today, they have a fragmented distribution along water courses, limited by fire and drought in one direction, seepage and flooding in the other.[16]

In Louisiana, the Mississippi River has shaped and reshaped the landscape; some of the state has conditions similar to those of coastal Florida, but it also features many areas with their own distinct characteristics. Among them are the chenier plain, prairies, swamplands, bayous, and pine flatlands. In each of these, live oaks play a different ecological role. At some time in the past, the trees may well have ranged north along the river valleys; live oaks grow on their own today in some forests as far north as the area around Melrose Plantation, just south of Natchitoches. How they got there is unclear.

The chenier plain of southwestern Louisiana is a large flat marshy region interrupted by old beach ridges of sand and shell that run parallel to the coast. The word "chenier" derives from the French name for oaks, *chêne*, and means "place of oaks," because live oaks are characteristic of these ridges. (The term can also refer to natural levee forests.) Cheniers range in size from a foot or two high, visible as a single row of oaks, to large areas several miles long, like Grand Chenier and Pecan Island. The typical forest cover is live oak and sugarberry or hackberry (*Celtis laevigata*), with mixtures of other trees and an understory that can include sabal palm and prickly pear. Cheniers are an important physical feature in the region: they protect inland marshes from saltwater incursions. They also provide crucial habitat for birds migrating across the Gulf of Mexico. In spring the oak-hackberry forests are their first resting place after a long flight. Exhausted warblers, vireos, flycatchers, and other songbirds crowd the area, staying to feed on the abundant insect life. In fall they stop over again, joining the monarch butterflies that mass in the oaks before heading south.

Live oaks nearest the coast are sculpted by the constant wind and salt spray. They often grow in crowded conditions. Huddling together for protection, becoming gnarled and twisted, they little resemble their magnificent inland cousins. Beneath their canopy, the forest is low and tangled, filled with mosquitoes and other insects appreciated by the birds (but not by the bird-watchers). Inland, live oaks become larger. On Grand Chenier, one of the largest forma-

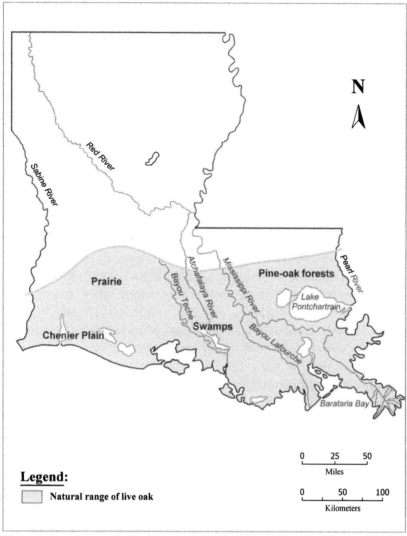

Map 3.4 *Natural distribution of live oaks in Louisiana. Map adapted from U.S. Forest Atlas of Trees.*

tions and one that has long been settled, are huge old trees, sometimes forming an open savanna with prickly pear and sabal palm where cattle graze.

Also within the chenier plain are several large salt domes, known as islands because they rise above the surrounding marshes. Avery Island, Jefferson Island, and Weeks Island are examples. All are home to live oaks. To the east along the coast are occasional true islands, like Grand Isle, where live oaks play a role in stabilizing the land and protecting settlements from the destructive force of hurricanes. It is possible these trees were deliberately brought there by people (see Chapter 4).

The broad floodplains associated with the major rivers in Louisiana (Mississippi, Red, Ouachita, Pearl, Tensas, Calcasieu, Sabine, and Atchafalaya) are covered in what is called "bottomland forest." It is anything but a uniform forest. Relatively small differences in elevation, created by abandoned river channels, natural levees, and meandering bayous, exert a precise and easily noticeable influence on vegetation patterns. When rivers and bayous flood their banks, they deposit coarse sediments first, creating a ridge, or levee, of well-drained soil that grades slowly into the poorly drained backswamp. Live oaks mark the upper section of the levees only, forming part of a linear forest type that follows the watercourses. It includes other kinds of oaks, hackberry, elm, ash, and dwarf palmetto.[17] The banks of Bayou Teche still have remnants of these oak associations. Although these stands would appear extensive to anyone traveling by water, in fact they do not represent much total area, since they are basically narrow ribbons of land within the vast swamp.

The best descriptions of live oaks in what is now Louisiana at the time of European contact were made by those looking for usable ship timber. In 1744, the French cartographer Bellin mapped an extensive area south of New Orleans, in the Barataria region, noting the "Bois de Chêneverd propre pour la construction" (forest of live oaks suitable for construction).[18] These oaks grew on islands within the swamp formed by river deposits. Usable trees were actually relatively scarce in the region at that time. In fact, the U.S. government was so concerned about future reserves for shipbuilding that in 1828 Cathcart and Landreth were sent to find live oak and other timber for the United States Navy in the swamps of Louisiana. They found significant stands in the Atchafalaya Basin, east of Bayou Teche. Not far from the town of Franklin, in "Grand Alias Chetimaches Lake," they discovered and named Cypress Island, about 299 hectares (739 acres) in area. They concluded that

upon an average this Island would produce at least four good Trees of Live Oak to an acre with fine large and valuable limbs for Ship building two of which Trees we measured and found them to be upwards of nine feet in diameter. Suppose there [were] thousand good Live Oak Trees on this Island and each Tree containing three Tons of Timber which is considerably below the mark. here on this Island would be nine thousand Tons of Live Oak Timber.[19]

Live oaks occupied only the driest portions of these islands. John Landreth describes the topography of Cypress Island as "most beautifully diversified by ridges and valleys running in a north Westerly and South Easterly direction across this Island the ridges about one hundred yards wide producing Live Oak . . . the valleys about twenty yards wide cypress of the largest class." The islands varied in age and size, as did the oaks growing on them. Some had much younger trees, referred to as "Nursery to the young Timber," and Landreth suggested that improving drainage and preventing floods would allow the trees to mature much faster. In some parts of the area they found little or no live oak. All together, the two explorers recommended 7,692 hectares (19,000 acres) on Commissioners, Cypress, and six islands in Lake Chetimaches be reserved, giving the navy access to thirty-seven thousand live oaks.[20]

John Landreth noted that within the whole area he had explored, frequent flooding killed off young live oaks and damaged mature trees. To prevent this, he suggested "banking and ditching wherever necessary . . . for I am well satisfied from observation that were this precaution made use of that all the Islands and Margins of Bayous where ever the Land was firm and Solid in this country would be well Set with young Live Oak and that it is much owing to the inundations of the waters of this country that this valuable Tree is so scarce."[21] Here is another indication that the live oak's habitat was limited, and changed frequently.

Live oaks were also relatively scarce to the west in the prairie area. These open grasslands were dissected by bayous lined with gallery forests. Widely spaced live oaks sometimes form a sort of savanna look in small sections of this region, but native stands are otherwise limited to occasional individuals along bayou levees, small clumps on raised "islands," and the so-called pimple mounds in the western part of the area.

North of Lake Pontchartrain, in northeastern Louisiana, is an entirely different kind of forest. Dominated by live oaks, longleaf, slash and loblolly pine, and southern magnolia, this association has also been called maritime forest and maritime mesophytic forest. Sandy, well-drained soils predominate, and fire and salt spray have had more influence on the vegetation than flooding. This forest is drier, more open, and lighter and has more varied topography than the swamps. Tall pines often tower over the live oaks, which either become understory trees or grow upright, with long leafless limbs reaching for light. Some of the state's largest, most magnificent live oaks are also here, including the Seven Sisters Oak in Lewisville, which is currently recognized as the largest live oak known. The southern border of this forest type is Lake Pontchartrain, where some live oaks grow right on the shore. Fontainbleau State Park has what may be a remnant of this association. To the north, it grades into pine forests.

In the early 1800s people feared the live oaks would all be gone within fifty to sixty years unless something was done to protect and encourage them. The overall impression of the species that emerges from these early accounts is of a tree that is highly adaptable yet particular in some requirements. It needs light and open habitats to get started—hurricane-ravaged land, periodically inundated natural levees, new islands of sand created by rivers, edges of lakes and fire-openings in pinelands are some likely spots. Once established, it can persist through later floods, high winds, and even saltwater spray and tidal inundations. But its roots cannot survive if permanently water-logged (as can those of the bald cypress or black gum), so that it can grow only on upper portions of the natural levees and the higher ground on islands. It was often a scruffy looking tree, only occasionally developing into the well-balanced specimen that represents the ideal landscape tree today.

Live oaks are important members of their various ecological communities. Countless birds nest in their branches and trunks; their importance in the chenier habitat has already been noted. Squirrels are an almost constant presence in live oaks, living among the branches and busily planting acorns in the fall. Timothy Silver, in his history of the South Atlantic forests, notes that bears roamed live oak woods of the coastal plains, and big flocks of turkeys used to live in live oak forests. Passenger pigeons ate enormous quantities of acorns. These nuts are still an important food for a wide range of birds including ducks, grouse, pheasant, pigeon, jays, grosbeaks, nuthatches, and woodpeckers. Other mammals that eat the acorns include beaver, fox, hare, muskrat, opossum, rabbit, raccoon, squirrel, chipmunks, and mice.[22]

Cultural Distribution

One major effect of the trees' popularity in the last hundred years has been a dramatic increase in its distribution. Today, live oaks can be seen planted in front of homes through most of Louisiana and even north into Arkansas. Map 3.3 shows some of the locations north of the species' natural range where I saw or heard reliable reports of live oaks, and a suggested cultural distribution in the Southeast. What the map does not show is how the trees have spread *within* their natural range into habitats formerly inaccessible. As people have drained wet areas and controlled flooding with ever-higher levees and have removed native forests from high ground, live oaks have moved into areas they could not have occupied earlier.

People also regularly move whole trees and acorns around. I have heard about live oaks brought from Texas to St. Francisville (which were probably Texas live oak, *Q. fusiformis*), from Mississippi to Church Point, from Grand Isle to other parts of Louisiana, and many from nearby forests to home and public properties within the state. Acorns from plantations in Alabama and other neighboring areas get planted at home, just as trees from Louisiana yield seed for dispersal to other regions. The effects on the genetics of the species are entirely unknown.

Life Cycle

For such a huge tree, the live oak produces surprisingly small, slim acorns. They are pointed and dark, with a count of about 558 to the kilogram (390 to the pound). Although in good years they cover the ground below the parent trees in a solid mass, few seem to sprout. Those not eaten quickly by a variety of wildlife soon become hollow; weevils bore their way in as soon as the acorns drop, devouring the sweet, rich food inside.

As seeds, the acorns are finicky and cannot be stored for longer than a few weeks without rotting. So eager are they to start growing that some fall off the tree with the radicle (the first root) already growing. The seeds need sandy, well-drained soil and plenty of water to germinate.

Once established, the young trees grow quickly and can easily be six feet tall in their third year. From the beginning they display their genetic variability. As Joey Billeaud, who grows thousands of live oaks each year at Live Oak Gardens, put it, "You're not going to find two live oaks that look very much alike." They vary in leaf shape, size and thickness, color, branching pattern, and how many of their leaves they shed in the winter months. Light intensity helps determine their form as they grow, but there is some genetic difference too—some tend to grow upward more than others.

Unlike most trees, the live oak has no single dominant growth point that suppresses growth of lateral buds. It is more likely to have three to five, or even fifty buds equally able to grow. Given full light, good soil, and plenty of moisture, a live oak will grow vigorously in all directions, forming a fountain shape, with limbs that eventually reach the ground and may even snake along the surface. Sometimes such spreading trees look like a group of seedlings that germinated at the same time (which can also happen). If one side is damaged by wind or salt spray, the trees assume fantastic shapes as they continue to grow in whatever direction is favorable. They can creep along with shifting sands. Limbs damaged by lightning, high winds, or deliberate pruning are generally replaced by vigorous new growth.

Sometimes the limbs reach lengths that defy laws of engineering. In a description of live oaks written in 1828, Judge Henry Brackenridge, who spent years observing the trees, wrote:

> One of these branches which I measured some years ago, I found seventy-five feet in length, and the extremity was so low, that I could reach it from the ground. From this peculiar habit, it rarely attains its full size anywhere except on the margins of rivers, on the shores of the bays and sounds, and on the edges of the open ponds, seldom extending any distance back, which I consider entirely owing to the[ir] being crowded by other trees, and consequently to the want of proper space.[23]

In shaded situations, the pattern changes. Trees growing close together will take an upright shape, or will angle toward the light. Tall, gangly trees result. Lower branches, deprived of light tend to drop off.

3.5 Pegleg, a live oak at Houmas House Plantation, demonstrates the species' ability to grow long horizontal branches that defy laws of engineering.

Live oak wood is the hardest and densest of all oaks. Its fibers are twisted and irregular. The live oak's growth form, tough wood, and ability to regrow after damage all contribute to its survival in the hurricane zone of the Gulf Coast. Its center of gravity is low, offering least resistance to the wind. The wood's structure allows it to bend and give during high winds, unlike other, more brittle, species that break under pressure. Live oak recovery from wind damage is remarkable. Paul Orr, Louisiana state urban forester, told me of four oaks in Morgan City that were completely stripped of leaves and small twigs by Hurricane Andrew in 1992. Two weeks later they had leafed out again and made a complete recovery the following year. During an earlier hurricane, several large oaks were uprooted, left lying on their sides, but after being pushed upright and reburied, they too survived.

The twisted grain and lack of well-defined growth rings make it impossible to accurately determine the age of trees, and getting an adequate core is a hopeless task. Despite the difficulty, figuring out the age of oaks is an obsession with some people, and their research has led to a better understanding of the trees' life span. Edwin Stephens, founder of the Live Oak Society (see Chapter 4), devised a method for estimating age based on circumference of the trunk. After measuring many oaks for years and comparing them to a tree with a known planting date, he concluded that in one hundred years a live oak would be 5.2 m (17 ft.) in circumference. After that it would increase at a rate of 1.3 cm (.5 in.) per year.[24] That system has been used as an estimate since then. However, Glenn Conrad, a historian and oak lover who has been monitoring live oaks for some time, believes that the rate of growth is much more variable than the earlier studies suggest. In his annual measurements of trees in New Iberia, he has found some relatively aged trees increasing at more than an inch a year while others hardly grow at all for many years. Other examples support his observations. The owners of Ambrosia Plantation in St. Francisville showed me a photo of the large grove of live oaks in front of the house taken in 1930, and it is clear they have not grown noticeably in the last sixty-five years. Those trees are growing in a dense stand, and are limited by competition for light and nutrients.

Climate and soil both exert a strong influence on growth rates and final size. Temperatures within the live oak's range go from 43.3° to -17.8° C (110° to 0° F); rainfall varies from .64 m (25 in.) at its western limit in Texas to 1.65 m (65 in.) along the eastern Gulf Coast. At their northern and western limits, trees never reach the sizes attained in southern Louisiana. For example, a live oak planted in a Tuscaloosa cemetery as a memorial in 1964 was only about 3.7 m (12 ft.) tall in 1994. While trees can survive frosts, hard freezes will split the bark and even the trunk, which then leads to disease and decay. Cold is thus a limiting factor inland and north; inadequate rainfall is a constraint in the west.

Live oak roots, thick and gnarled, are often prominent above ground. Underground, they can extend two and a half times as far as the canopy, much farther than the commonly believed limit at the canopy edge. Feeder roots are shallow, confined to the top 25 cm (10 in.) of soil. Tree expert Jim Foret has found that some also have anchor roots, a completely different kind of root that is thick and solid, like a wedge going straight down to help hold the top firm. Another variation is that some trees appear to be growing up on a mound. Experts don't agree on the cause. One theory says it is the result of soil around them compacting and eroding, leaving the roots exposed; another suggests it is a growth form that is genetically determined. When a tree is cut or girdled or suffers some other serious damage, sprouts grow from the root crown and surface roots. Stressed trees often have a veritable thicket of young shoots carpeting the ground. Because of persistent roots, killing a live oak can be a challenge. Sometimes, if the main trunk of an older tree is entirely removed, it sends up a new main shoot that will grow rapidly, fed by the established root system.

Although people like to believe live oaks are five hundred years old or more, even the most venerable giants are probably two to three hundred years old, according to botanists and tree specialists who have worked with this species. Much about the live oak's way of life seems mysterious to humans. Hollow oaks fascinate people, as do fallen trees that continue to live for many years. Live oaks can live for many years without any heartwood, since the transfer of water and nutrients happens in the ring of annually renewed cambium. Sometimes limbs rot and suddenly fall for no apparent reason (usually the result of sudden temperature changes that cause an already dead limb to crack). But even if half a tree falls, the other half often lives. As they age, some trees develop great burls. Again, I was offered two explanations—either they're an indication of great age or the result of a virus.

Live oak canopies are similar to tropical rainforest canopies in that they are whole complex ecosystems. Paul Orr, who has spent a lot of time climbing around in live oaks as part of his urban forestry job, has found earthworms in the canopy, thriving in decaying leaves and other organic matter that has gathered among the great limbs. There often is enough of this material to allow other plant seeds to germinate, including those of other trees like magnolia.

Live oaks are also host to a wide range of epiphytes. Most cause no harm, merely using the branches as support, obtaining nutrients from the air and captured detritus. Spanish moss (*Tillandsia usneoides*) is the best known of these. A member of the bromeliad family of flowering plants, Spanish moss used to be plentiful on live oaks and other trees of southern Louisiana. Birds spread seeds and portions of the plants from tree to tree. Much of the Spanish moss was destroyed by a disease that spread through the region; some blame its decline on air pollution. A related *Tillandsia*, ball moss, has become a problem for trees in cultivation. Unlike Spanish moss, this plant forms dense clumps that surround twigs and branches and block the light.

Resurrection fern (*Polypodium polypodioides*) cascades down the main trunk and branches, following the path of water during rainfalls. Its lush green fronds turn into inconspicuous brown curls between rains, only to turn green again within hours of the next rainfall. More elusive and hard to find are green fly orchids (*Epidendrum conopseum*). Many trees also sport various other lichens and mosses. Some are benign, while others indicate slow growth, which can signal decay.

Remarkably few pests or diseases bother live oaks. Oak wilt (*Ceratocystis fagacearum*) is a major problem among live oaks in Texas, where it spreads rapidly through the root systems of the clonal Texas live oak, *Q. fusiformis*. That disease has not yet had a major effect on Louisiana's live oaks. But the recent discovery of extensive damage from Formosan termites in the oaks of New Orleans live oaks has urban foresters and citizens worried. This Asian species has been in the area for at least fifty years, but damage to trees wasn't noticed until after Hurricane Andrew swept through, when many of the downed live oaks were found to be infested. However, New Orleans and Louisiana state foresters have both concluded that the main danger from these termites is to old wooden buildings—healthy live oak wood is too tough for the pests.

Comparisons

Both ceibas and live oaks belong to genera that are highly significant to people over much of the world, *Ceiba* in tropical regions and *Quercus* in the temperate and subtropical regions. Each is the largest or among the largest trees in its region. Some trees might grow taller than a live oak, but no species rivals it in sheer volume, size of trunk, and area shaded. The huge old cypresses of the swamps of Louisiana once might have dwarfed a live oak, but they are long gone. Ceiba, being emergents in the tropical rainforests, are clearly among the tallest, while those in plazas are among the widest, trees known. Among the many tree species in their regions, these two stand out. Both inhabit the same places people favor. In Louisiana, live oaks perch on high ground within the miles of swampy lowlands; ceibas in Guatemala mark rivers and other water sources in dry climate regions.

Both trees seem designed for life with people. In fact, both might be considered weeds. Both produce abundant seed, and can do so even if only one tree is present in an area. Ceibas can reproduce from parts of the parent plant; live oak resprouts from roots. Both are pioneer species, able to invade disturbed habitat, and in fact require open areas to germinate and become established. Since creating disturbance is one of humankind's most popular activities everywhere, ceibas and live oaks have reaped the benefits of new lands to colonize. Both species also tolerate a wide range of soil and moisture conditions, enabling them to accompany people into many ecosystems.

Sheer persistence and adaptability are other qualities shared by ceibas and live oaks. Both grow quickly and can persist for hundreds of years. Ceibas' huge buttresses and live oaks' tough wood protect them from high winds and even hurricanes, while also making cutting them difficult. Since neither is valued for its timber today, it is often easier to let them be and plan around them than cut them down. Both trees respond to physical damage by regrowing vigorously. That means they can be shaped by people pruning them and can survive the almost inevitable damage that plants suffer when living in the midst of people. Neither tree provides an easy way to determine its true age, thus defying scientific measurement.

Because of their long life and huge size, both trees become entire ecosystems, homes for other species of plants and animals. The vast area of their shade creates a distinctive microclimate, important in the hot climates to which both are native. Their extensive branches and roots provide locations for nests, burrows, and perches. Live oaks yield abundant acorns that feed a wide range of birds and mammals, while ceiba flowers are an important source of pollen and nectar. Epiphytes of the families Bromeliaceae and Orchidaceae, along with ferns, are common and numerous on both. The presence of a single tree in the forest or in the midst of human settlement therefore has a large effect on the ecology of the area.

A major difference is the quality of their wood: ceiba wood is so light and porous that it is considered useful only for things like plywood, whereas live oak is so hard and difficult to work that getting rid of old trees is a major problem. Another difference is their shape when growing in the wild. Live oaks, given adequate room and light, have a drooping, sprawling form. Ceibas shoot for the sky, with a long straight bole. Yet both are remarkably adaptable to less than ideal conditions, and both recover from damage rapidly. In their native forest habitats both species are relatively scarce in numbers, but the live oak often grows in groves, dominating certain kinds of forest communities, while ceibas are more frequently solitary, spread widely in the native forests. Both ceibas and live oaks have long been brought into cultivation and introduced into areas they would never have reached on their own. They are easy to transplant when young, growing quickly into specimens that look old. Within a human generation, they can be large enough to begin collecting legends.

Chapter 4

CULTURAL HISTORY

HOW TREES DEVELOP CHARACTER

THE STORIES of how ceibas and live oaks became so important to their human companions form a tapestry composed of many strands. Like other trees important in landscapes throughout the world, these two species carry layers of cultural symbolism, individual histories, and community memories. Through time and space, their roles have changed, and humans have made decisions and told tales that affected landscapes for years to come. The trees, meanwhile, have responded to changing conditions in their own ways, thus contributing to the evolving story. As I sorted through the historical literature on ceibas and live oaks, and compared it to observations from fieldwork within various cultural contexts, several distinct personalities emerged for each tree. Tracing the history of each of these proved to be a useful way to better understand how they have come to be such dominant features of their respective landscapes. But while one or another of these personalities has dominated at specific times and places, I would emphasize that no single personality predominates. Human-tree relationships are far too ancient and complex to reduce to one dimension.

CEIBA

Throughout its range in three major world regions, the ceiba has been singled out as extraordinary. Within Guatemala, the ceiba is remarkable for having survived as symbolic through many centuries of conquest and different worldviews and rulers. Human focus on this tree species is working to ensure that it continues to be planted and protected through much of the nation.

Sacred Tree of the Maya

Along the entrance road to the ruins of Tikal, in the Petén lowlands of Guatemala, grows a straight, tall-trunked ceiba with well-defined buttresses (see Fig. 3.1). A sign at its base announces in Spanish that this is "Ceiba (Maya Yaxche)." It goes on to explain that the Maya believed this was the tree of life, and therefore only priests and nobles were allowed to wear clothing made from the fibers of its fruits. The ceiba's branches were believed to hold up the sky, and after death, Mayans would rest forever in the shade of a ceiba.

All visitors to Tikal walk by this sign. Many don't notice it at all. Some stop to read it, and a few go up to touch the tree or stand among its roots for a photograph of *el árbol nacional.* It is the only *Ceiba pentandra* they will see so identified. In fact, there are very few ceibas obvious about the ruins. The sign itself sounds straightforward—but who exactly are the Maya to whom it refers? Does it mean only the people of the classic era who built the great pyramids and ball courts of Tikal? What of the highland Maya, or the 45 million people in Guatemala today who speak one of the Mayan languages?

As a culture group, the Maya go back to at least 2000 B.C. They lived, and continue to live, in a geographical area that extends from the lowlands of the Yucatán peninsula and the Petén, throughout the highlands of southern Mexico, Guatemala, and El Salvador, and along the Pacific coastal plain south into Honduras. For more than thirty-five hundred years before Europeans arrived in Middle America, the Maya developed several phases of sophisticated urban centers in different parts of this region. They also controlled much of the trade between areas to the north and south and had regular contact with the Aztecs in later times.

For the people who first settled the tropical rainforests of Middle America, trees were the source of food, medicine, wood, shade, and shelter. Ceibas supplied a number of products: their wood, being so soft, was easy to shape into canoes; the young pods were edible; the silk floss of the mature fruit made an excellent stuffing material and was reportedly spun into a cloth in some regions; the seeds when boiled yield an oil useful in cooking and lighting. Different parts of the tree have been used as medicine: leaves to treat swellings, burns, and rashes; roots as a diuretic; the bark to heal ulcerations, hemorrhoids, and gonorrhea, and to start menstrual flow and expel placentas. An extract of the bark has been shown to act on the central nervous system in a manner similar to that of curare. Drinking the sap of the tree is supposed to help a person gain weight (and if it goes too far, one cuts the tree down to reverse the effect). Among the Huastec in Veracruz, the bark is still used for treating measles.[1]

Ceibas also have an association with water. In the Yucatán, they often grow near cenotes, water sources within the dry karst landscapes that have long been centers of villages and sacred rituals. Their presence is in fact an indicator of water near the surface. Their frequent presence near rivers also enhances their connection to places where human life is possible.

The main information available about the ceiba as a sacred tree is from the classic Maya period (A.D. 300–900). By that time it was already a highly developed symbol of the world tree, or *axis mundi*. The Mayan name for ceiba is *yaxche*. Translated it becomes *yax* = the, the first, the blue-green; and *che* = tree. In Mayan plant classification *yax*, or blue-green, is the most important, the first color; its association with the ceiba is an indication of its central role as a symbolic tree. According to Linda Schele and Paul Freidel, in their book *A Forest of Kings*,

> Running through this center, the Maya envisioned an axis called *Wacah Chan* ("six sky" or "raised up sky"). The tree which symbolized this axis coexisted in all three vertical domains. Its trunk went through the Middleworld; its roots plunged to the nadir in the watery Underworld region of the Otherworld, and its branches soared to the zenith in the highest layer of the heavenly region of the Otherworld.[2]

Ceibas were portrayed symbolically in several ways; one was on the carved stones known as stelae, or tree stones. When they erected monuments and stelae, according to Schele and Freidel, the Maya were recreating the essential components of their sacred geography: mountains, forest, and cave. This last was the temple itself, at the summit of the pyramid. It was surrounded by four deep holes into which the builders inserted four tree trunks that represented the four

4.1 Carved upright stones at Mayan ruins, or stelae, form image of the world tree.

sacred trees of the cardinal directions. In some temples these were ceiba trunks.

The king, as chief priest, became the world tree when he conducted bloodletting ceremonies necessary to sustain life.

On public monuments, the oldest and most frequent manner in which the king was displayed was in the guise of the World Tree. Its trunk and branches were depicted on the apron covering his loins, and the Double-headed Serpent Bar that entwined in its branches was held in his arms. The Principal Bird Deity . . . at its summit was rendered as his headdress.[3]

The close connection between people and ceibas is demonstrated in this image, as well as the power inherent in natural objects. Ceibas were places of power associated with those who had both political and religious authority. Another sign of their importance is that several groups claim direct descent from the ceiba, including the Lacandon and the Tzeltales.

The tree had a distinctly feminine side. One was maternal: young children who died were cared for by a ceiba, which fed them milk from its breast-like fruits. As a symbol of abundance, the ceiba was also connected to Imix, the name of the first day of the Mayan calendar. A darker aspect was the X-tabai, a beautiful woman all dressed in white who lurked among the roots. She tempted men to their death if they wandered nearby at night. This belief persists in the Yucatán, but was not familiar to Guatemalans I spoke with in the highlands.[4]

The ceiba as world tree was sometimes shown as a cross, an image that had important consequences when the Spanish arrived with the Christian cross. The similarities in symbolism often helped in the conversion of Mayan people, since raising the cross was similar to setting up a symbolic ceiba. In some areas, a cross painted green is still worshipped.[5]

Among the Aztecs the ceiba was symbolic, too. They called the ceiba *pochotl* (from which the contemporary name "pochote" derives). The following entry from the Florentine Codex, for example, emphasizes its association with power and the value placed on the tree's shade:

Silk Cotton Tree (Ceiba pentandra; pochotl)
It is smooth, smooth in all parts; dense; quite circular, well

rounded, quite rounded; shady, shadowy. It shades; it gives shade, it gives shadow; it shades one. Under it, one is shaded. Hence, for this reason, it is called "the governor"; for he becomes [as] a silk cotton tree, a cypress.[6]

The word *"pochotl"* has a distinct resemblance to the word *"pochteca,"* which refers to the class of professional traders within Aztec society who traveled throughout Middle America. Geographer Bill Davidson, who has been fascinated with ceiba distribution for years, suggested the similarity in the two words may reflect the strong link between ceibas and travel. Ceibas often do mark river crossings, travel routes, road intersections, and marketplaces. Early Spanish accounts of Central America also describe markets held in the shade of ceiba trees. Oviedo y Valdez, traveling in Nicaragua in the 1520s, wrote of the ceiba that it

> is unimportant except for two things: One is its wool and the other its vast shade, for the branches are very wide-spreading, and the shade is wholesome, not oppressive like that of other trees of the Indies, which is notoriously harmful . . . The Indians of Nicaragua have places set aside for the *tianguez* or market, and there they have two, three, or four of these ceyba trees for shade, which are sufficient to shelter one to two thousand people . . . In the province of Nicaragua this tree is called *poxot*, and in other places it has other names.[7]

Markets were central for economic as well as social and religious activities in the region. Generations of traders would have done business in the shade of such long-lived trees. The taller trees were also excellent landmarks for travelers, visible at great distances. The town of La Ceiba in Honduras was long known for several tall ceibas along the coast that marked the place where traders could bring bananas and other crops to market.

An old Guatemalan story gives a different explanation for the name pochotl. It links the ceiba with a god, Pochuta, whose name comes from the world "fat," referring to his corpulent stature. This friendly god, actually a demi-god, led the people away from the dangers of a world destroyed by the gods of hurricanes and earthquakes. He became the pochuta tree that still guards communities throughout the area. Yet another derivation of pochotl or pochutl is that it means "protector."[8]

In some areas of Guatemala, people use the name pochote for *Ceiba aesculifolia*. In Yucatecan Maya that tree is called *pi'im*. Archeological evidence from the ancient Mayan center of Coba in the Yucatán suggests pi'im was cultivated as a fiber crop there. It had ceremonial importance; only the higher classes were allowed to use it. They may have cultivated large numbers of trees on land near the centers of settlements.[9]

Shamans conducted their rituals by ceiba trees, often using incense to prepare trees for sacred ceremonies. These practices continued well into the Christian era. Bishop Cortés y Larraz, on his trip to visit priests in the province of Guatemala in 1769, was disturbed to find the native people still practicing their old religion; he noted that when conducting healing rituals the *curanderos* took their patients to ceibas in the forest, where they lit candles and burned incense as they invoked the name of their "heathen" gods. A hundred years later, Karl Sapper, in his travels to the Pacific coast in the nineteenth century, noted that large ceibas still received gifts from local people. This practice probably continues; several Guatemalan tour guides said they knew of particular ceibas on the Pacific coast and in the Petén still honored in the old ways. The Lacandon are said to visit the trees at the ruins of Sayaxché. Most references suggest the chosen trees are primarily wild-growing individuals, although one person I spoke with said he had seen offerings among the roots of a lowland plaza tree.[10]

Mayan settlements in the lowlands often clustered around ceiba trees. In his book on travels in Guatemala in 1878–1883, the German geographer Otto Stoll has a sketch entitled "Der Heilige Baum der Maya" (the sacred tree of the Maya). It shows a traditional Mayan village of thatched huts in a circle centered on a large ceiba tree. Were such trees planted? The Maya have been accomplished agriculturists for thousands of years, so it was certainly within their abilities. In the 1930s, anthropologist Robert Redfield recorded ritual plantings of ceibas in Yucatán villages for certain festivals. He noted that this could have derived from European as well as indigenous customs. However, a contemporary Guatemalan ethnobotanist, Edgar Geovany Mendoza, believes it highly unlikely that any traditional Maya of the past would have planted living ceiba trees in their villages. The sacred ceiba is one found in the forest, he told me, chosen because it is in a sacred location near water or a cave, or because of its appearance (a swollen trunk, for instance, can suggest a pregnant woman). Within the lowland tropics such trees were so common in the forests and clearings that planting them would make no sense. However, once an area was cleared, ceibas would likely seed naturally near human habitations, and, if protected, grow to maturity. The rapid growth of the trees no doubt played a part in their role as a symbol of abundance.[11]

Even if the early Maya did not plant ceibas in pre-Conquest times, they did influence the distribution and abundance of wild-growing ceibas. During classic Mayan times, settlement throughout the Petén lowlands was relatively dense, and intensive agriculture affected most, if not all, of the forests at some time. The same was true of the Pacific lowlands. Given the trees' ability to produce large quantities of highly mobile seeds, and their invasive tendencies, ceibas would take advantage of any open sites resulting from forest clearing. Frequently mentioned in both older and current accounts of the region is that people (especially Mayans) do not like to cut ceiba trees, and will leave them when clearing forests. That gives the trees an even greater advantage for survival and seed dispersal. (Cutting ceibas has also become illegal, since it is the national tree.)

What of today's Maya? Is the ceiba still considered sacred? That depends on whom you ask. The highland peoples I met and talked with have a range of ideas concerning the ceiba. Some Mayan speakers don't recognize a ceiba at all. Several women told me it was just a tree, like all the others. A few spoke about ceibas that once grew in their villages. Schoolchildren, though, know it was the sacred tree of the Maya and also the national tree, because this is a regular part of their education. In highland Mayan villages I found examples of young ceibas entirely ignored, while others were carefully marked and respected. Large trees are more generally known and valued. The tree of Palín is carefully watched over by the women, who consider it a gift from the ancestors who planted it. In the lowlands, there appears to be a much more general awareness of ceibas. However, practical considerations can take over. A Peace Corps worker who had lived and worked with Kekchi (Maya) colonizers of the lower slopes of the Polochic Valley said they regularly cut down young ceiba trees that were invading their cornfields.

Complicating the picture are several other belief systems that have influenced the ceiba's status as sacred. Trees on plazas are auto-

4.2 The Basilica of Esquipulas, home of the Black Christ and a major pilgrimage site, features a ceiba tree with whitewashed trunk.

matically associated with the Catholic Church. But there are also plenty of examples of ceibas deliberately planted next to churches outside of plazas. In Palín, for example, the church at the edge of town, El Calvario, has its own ceiba. It was not surprising to learn that the Basilica of Esquipulas, home of the Black Christ and a major pilgrimage site of Middle America, has a ceiba (Fig. 4.2). A well-kept tree, its trunk shines with fresh white paint that matches the impressive basilica. What did surprise me was that it was planted by an American, one of the Benedictine monks from Louisiana who live there. The grounds around the basilica used to be open, until this man decided to create a garden behind the structure and to plant trees in front. The ceiba seemed a natural. There are four more planted at a nearby bridge. Bill Davidson told me he had been asked by Mayan pilgrims to take photographs of them in front of that ceiba.

On the Caribbean coast, African belief systems concerning the ceiba may have merged with indigenous customs. The ceiba tree, as noted in Chapter 3, is also native to Africa and is highly significant to a number of groups there. Among the Beng of West Africa, for instance, no village is a suitable place to live until a ceiba has been planted in the center. In Jamaica, many of African descent consider the ceiba a shrine, a place to communicate with the spirits, both good and evil, who dwell in the tree. The cemetery ceiba with the big snake in Livingston, Guatemala, sounds like another possible example of diffusion of beliefs.[12]

Valuing a particular tree as a representative of the world tree, where communication with other worlds or gods is possible, is different from considering all members of a species as sacred objects or beings. Current laws protecting ceibas from being cut derive from this species definition, a way of thinking that may or may not be part of how others conceive the world. I also believe there was always a difference in attitudes and beliefs regarding the ceiba between highland and lowland Maya. Among the upland Maya, a flowering mountain is the image that defines life, a much more appropriate one for that region. Considering their complex history as a culture group, to assume any kind of uniformity in attitudes toward ceiba trees among all the Maya is unrealistic.

Plaza Trees

Like the history of the plaza itself, the story of plaza ceibas shows the blending of cultural patterns, and how trees and humans together create symbolic images that in turn affect the tree's cultural meaning.[13] The ceiba of Palín is Guatemala's best-known ceiba today. Fifty years ago, the ceiba of Jocotenango was the exemplary ceiba, featured on the cover of a book compiled to celebrate the new national symbol. It, too, grew in a plaza, in a town next to Guatemala City.

The Spanish, when they arrived in the sixteenth century, quickly grasped the central importance of the ceiba to inhabitants of Middle America and made use of it for their own ends. Bernal Díaz del Castillo, in his firsthand account of the conquest of Mexico, reported that when Cortés arrived in Tabasco, on the Río de Grijalva, in 1519, he defeated the natives, then "took possession of the country in the King's name by drawing his sword and making three cuts in a great ceiba tree which stood in the central plaza of the town." Later, "a cross was made in a large ceiba tree on the spot where the battle was fought, in order to afford a long memorial thereof, for this tree has the quality of preserving scars on its bark."[14]

Other famous events of the conquest are also said to have taken place in the shade of large, central ceibas. Pedro de Alvarado cried under the foliage of a ceiba in the plaza of Masahuat, El Salvador, after his defeat by the Pasacos. Cuauhtémoc, the last Aztec emperor, and two faithful companions were hanged from a ceiba after their defeat in 1522. When the Spanish burned sacred Mayan books in Mani, Yucatán, they chose a spot near the sacred tree for the destruction.[15]

Appropriating cultural symbols has long been the practice of conquerors. The Spanish used the ceiba's role in traditional settlements to further their aims. Pre-conquest villages in the lowlands often had homes grouped around a central ceiba (see Stoll, footnote 11). Formal urban centers like Tikal and Copán had their tree stones. The Spanish, when choosing locations for forced resettlements, their way of keeping control over the population, often looked for large ceibas. Carlos V of Spain, according to Polonsky Celcer, is supposed to have encouraged this.

La ceiba aparece en nuestra historia como fundadora de pueblos, al conjuro de sus ramas se congregaba la gente y su exten-
dida sombra abre el ámbito de las plazas públicas; puede
decirse que es el primer edificio, el centro de la población, y
por esta circunstancia Carlos V dictó una disposición para que
se fundasen los pueblos en torno de una ceiba, sabedor de que
congregaba a las gentes y amparaba tradicionalmente a los
mercados.[16]

(The ceiba appears in our history as founder of towns; under
the spell of its branches the people gathered and its extensive
shade opens the limits of the public plazas; one could say it is
the first building, the center of the community, and for that
reason, Carlos V dictated a decree that towns should be
founded around a ceiba, knowing that it gathered people and
traditionally protected the markets.)

This was a particularly effective strategy in the lowlands, where such
large trees grew. But what of regions above a thousand meters, where
ceibas did not grow on their own? The Spanish may have started the
practice of planting ceibas deliberately in town centers. As noted
earlier, the Maya were perfectly capable of doing that, but probably
refrained because of the tree's sacred character, a powerful entity
to be respected. The Spaniards, of course, would not have had
such reservations. Later historians such as Polonsky Celcer credited
the conquerors for this custom and suggested it was done for noble
reasons.

Los conquistadores españoles, queriendo conservar aquella
hermosa tradición, aquel respeto por los símbolos de nuestros
antepasados, representados en esta simbólica planta, la sem-
braron en todas la plazas cerca de los cabildos, en todos los
sitios conquistados, junto al símbolo sacrosanto de la religión
cristiana: la sagrada Cruz y el Templo santo.

(The conquistadors, wanting to conserve that beautiful tradition, with respect for the symbols of our ancestors, represented in this symbolic plant, planted it in all the plazas near the
town offices, in all the areas conquered, next to the sacrosanct
symbol of the Christian religion, the sacred cross and the holy
church.)[17]

There is evidence that by the eighteenth century, at least, the Spanish had planted ceibas in plazas of Indian towns. When the villagers of Jocotenango were relocated (forcefully) from the outskirts of Antigua to the new capital, Guatemala City, in 1769, the Spanish-speaking rulers planted a ceiba in the new location (also called Jocotenango). This tree later became the center of the annual Festival of Jocotenango, which drew Indians from all over Guatemala each August. Batres Jáuregui, a Guatemalan writer, described vividly how during his childhood in the late nineteenth century the tree was transformed each year into an altar, covered with offerings of fruits and vegetables. Since then, the city has swallowed the town, turning it into part of the large urban complex. The ceiba is now gone. In the 1990s, the former center of celebration was a small, unremarkable square planted to pines. Hidden among them was one unobtrusive young ceiba, identified by a sign as the national tree.[18]

In the nineteenth century, Spanish-style plazas with ceibas were a familiar sight. The trees were appreciated for their shade in both Mayan and non-Mayan communities. It's unclear just how common such plaza trees were, however. A list of eight trees famous for their size appears in Polonsky-Celcer's 1962 *Monografía Antológica del Árbol: Palín, Amatitlán, Jocotenango, Palencia, San Francisco Petén, La Democracia, Escuintla, and Chiquimula.* Had many others died by then?

My search for the eight ceibas showed that at least half of them have died. Their stories remain. In Amatitlán, a resort town outside the capital (and just above the ceiba's natural range), a long dispute raged in the nineteenth century over who had planted the famous ceiba in town. Ernesto Chinchilla Aguilar settled this in his history of the town. According to his account, it was planted in 1835 by the poet known as La Pepita and her mother. La Pepita later enjoyed its shade and dedicated some lines of poetry to the tree.[19] The ceiba of Palencia, I discovered on my trip there, had been dead for twenty to thirty years. Escuintla's had been taken down by town officials. The trees in Palín, San Francisco, and La Democracia were still thriving in the mid-1990s. The ceiba in Chiquimula is also still growing according to reports from residents (I only glimpsed it briefly from a bus).

What accounts for the discrepancy between the commonly held belief that all towns used to have ceibas and the obviously ceiba-less towns all over Guatemala? Assuming they used to be there, what might have happened to them? Although people like to believe ceibas live five hundred years or more, a life span of two to three hundred years is more generally accepted by botanists. Any planted during the early colonial period, until about 1750 or 1800, could well have died of old age. Others have been removed because of changing fashions, as suggested by Escuintla's ceiba. Plazas have gone through different styles. At first they were open areas of soil or grass (with or without a ceiba). In the nineteenth century, plantings were introduced and the plazas became green. Eventually they included walkways, fountains, benches, and formal plantings of roses and clipped shrubs. This helps distinguish the area as civilized, distinct from the wild monte outside the town. Another possibility is that ceibas in plazas were never a universal pattern, but rather an ideal that harks back to how life used to be in the lowlands, where people naturally grouped their villages around a powerful tree.

Another major puzzle concerns the ceibas' shapes. In plazas, they most often assume a spreading shape, often much wider than they are tall, while wild-grown trees tend toward the vertical (compare the ceibas shown in Figures 1.1 and 3.1). I believe the plaza shape results from both internal and external factors. It is a product of human-tree relationships. Planted in an open spot, away from other trees, ceibas are more subject to wind and other severe events like lightning that can destroy the dominant growth point and force lateral growth. They have other stresses to contend with as well. Buildings and pavement can constrict their roots, and constant foot traffic compacts the soil. This affects tree growth. Children climbing young trees (and they will do that in spite of the thorns) can also damage the growth point, whether by accident or on purpose. The tree in Jocotenango (next to Antigua) is an example (Figure 2.5). In spite of the distress expressed by the town's custodian, the tree will probably be fine, just not tall. Finally, there is the question of deliberate pruning to create a spreading tree. While most people who lived near such trees accepted their shape as natural, a few Guatemalans told me that of course people pruned the trees to keep them from getting too tall. After all, explained Francisco Cane Acosta, my guide at Tikal, the point is to have shade.

National Tree of Guatemala

A campaign to have the ceiba named Guatemala's national tree was started early in the twentieth century by Dr. Sixto Padilla, a botanist from El Salvador. He called the ceiba the most important member of the flora, the most beautiful, the most intimately tied to the history of the country, and the largest of all the native trees. It wasn't until 1955 that another ceiba lover, Ulises Rojas, succeeded in this quest. On March 8 that year, a decree was issued from the national palace in Guatemala City, that henceforth the ceiba would be the *árbol nacional*. It joined two other living symbols of the country: the rare, almost extinct, quetzal is the national bird, and the monja blanca, an endangered orchid, is its official flower.[20] The choice of ceiba can be construed in several ways. One is an attempt to forge a sense of unity in a nation long divided along ethnic lines. The stress on the ceiba as the sacred tree of the Maya suggests that Indians and their values are being recognized. Of course the usual statement is that it was the sacred tree, implying it no longer is or that the Maya are no longer. Another interpretation is that this is another example of appropriating a powerful symbol, a way for the (non-Mayan) government to gain legitimacy, just as the Spanish did earlier by creating forced settlements around this tree.

Shortly after the decision that set the ceiba apart as different from other trees came the publication of *Monografía Antológica del Árbol*, mentioned earlier. Ceibas are representatives of nature, it says in the introduction. Stories of famous tress, the role of trees in human life, and essays on how to plant and care for trees fill the volume, along with photos and poems. The book outlines plans to plant ceibas in all public plazas and announces that people must be educated about trees, starting with the ceiba.

The tree's status as national symbol has brought it into the national consciousness in a new way. It has become not just a symbol of the nation but a tool for environmental education. Images of the ceiba are part of every schoolchild's learning, reproduced not only in textbooks and special pamphlets but also in national newspapers. During my first trip to Palín, in the company of a Guatemalan family, a nine-year-old girl recited a long and complicated lesson she had learned about ceibas. I had just arrived, and my Spanish was a little fuzzy, but I heard words like mountains, rainforest, streams, quetzal,

4.3 Newspaper inserts remind children of Guatemala of the nation's symbols, including the ceiba, the monja blanca (a native orchid), and the rare quetzal.

and electricity. Eventually I worked out that she had been learning that ceibas live in the rainforest, which must be protected to keep quetzals safe and also make sure the hydroelectric dams can work to provide electricity for those in the city. When I asked another young person about the ceiba in his town, Ciudad Vieja, he kept repeating something about *ceiba d'oro*, the ceiba of gold. That too, was puzzling, until I learned it was the name of a prize given to journalists, often mentioned on television.

Proyecto Guauhitemala, a group of people dedicated to preserving the country's forests, have published a series of books on the trees of Guatemala. Guauhitemala is a Nahuatl name that means "place of the forest." The first tree featured is the ceiba. In spite of the fact that it is now illegal to cut ceibas without a government permit, people on the coast continue to cut the trees for use as flooring.[21]

Juana, my Spanish teacher, reported on an unusual form of the national tree being sold at a nursery show in Antigua one year: bonsai ceibas. They sold for Q100, or about $17. I suspect this was an example of creative marketing. Some of the philodendron family have leaves that resemble the ceiba's. Once a young girl proudly showed me her aunt's "ceiba." If those bonsai were true ceibas, it would represent a remarkable transformation of the national symbol into a toy version of itself.[22]

In the coming years, it will be interesting to watch what happens with the many younger ceibas that have been planted all over the country, from highland villages to the Petén lowlands. Two have been planted in the most central symbolic plaza of all, that in Guatemala City. Others line the entrance road to Guatemala from Mexico, and ceibas grace the airport entrance in Guatemala City. Will this new wave of ceibas grow tall or broad? Will someone nip their central buds to encourage branching? Will they survive in urban centers, where air pollution may prove a problem? What will happen as their roots begin to heave the pavement around them?

Home and Community

Almost all the ceibas I found were in public places—in plazas, by churches, at entrances, and on roadsides. The exceptions were those in pastures and other privately held plantation lands within the tree's

4.4 *Young ceiba growing in Guatemala's symbolic center of power, the Guatemala City plaza. Photo by William V. Davidson.*

native range, and the few planted near private homes. These latter were homes of the wealthy, the only ones who had enough land to support such an enormous tree.

Given the land situation in Guatemala, this is not surprising. The vast majority of people own little or no land. Much of the coastal lowlands are now vast plantations of sugar, cotton, or bananas. Mid-slopes are devoted to coffee and a few other export crops. In the higher regions are more individual holdings, where people grow corn and other foods in small milpas. Even higher are grazing lands for sheep. Average plots are small, often not enough to feed the families that depend on them. Although small-scale flower plantings and container gardens are popular, as well as pocket gardens in tiny front yards, there is little of what would be called "landscaping" except on private estates of rich landowners and in the public areas of cities.

Even if people had land, would they choose to put in a ceiba? Juana, who became fascinated with the ceiba research as we continued to confer over several years, decided she wanted one in her backyard. Her husband refused, reminding her there would be no room for jocotes, their favorite fruit. A single ceiba overwhelms any piece of land it occupies. Last I knew, Juana was collecting ceiba seeds from the coast and trying to get them started along a street in her town. That seems to be the general feeling about ceibas—they belong in public. If they symbolize home, they mean a community, like Palín, not private land.

Travel Routes

Large ceibas are striking along many roads of Guatemala, as they are in other countries in this region. Their distinctive shapes and size make them easy to recognize. Often they mark intersections, and are further distinguished by their painted trunks and various signs. Many are one-sided or otherwise affected by growing near a major highway. Nevertheless, they are imposing.

Geographer Bill Davidson got so interested in ceibas along the Motagua valley road that he mapped them. They tended to be on the outside curves of the highway, he found, as if placed there deliberately. Bridges were another favorite site. Their presence in both these locations may well indicate continuity with ancient Mayan, Aztec, and perhaps earlier customs of marking travel routes. A tall ceiba, if felled correctly, makes an excellent bridge across rivers. It might also serve as a marker for travel routes or where crossing is possible.

The ceiba's natural habitat is along rivers and other disturbed sites; the tree's presence there is not a surprise. Roadsides provide an ideal open habitat for young seeds to germinate, assuming they also find sufficient water and nutrients. Getting there is certainly no problem. Whether planted there deliberately or allowed to grow once started, ceibas seem to do well in this situation.

Roadside ceibas make convenient locations for bus stops, police checkpoints, and eating establishments. Their shade is appreciated by travelers. In Guatemala City one of the main bus stops is still sheltered by an old ceiba.

Wild-Growing Trees Today

Ceibas growing spontaneously are still plentiful in Guatemala. In fact, in the lowlands of the Pacific coast, they are so ubiquitous that people will seldom buy one at a nursery. Anyone from the highlands who wants to plant a ceiba knows where to find one. Yet several people expressed their concern over the future of the ceiba in Guatemala. The rainforests everywhere are under pressure for agricultural land. When the road was put through on the coast, many ceibas and other trees were cut, and new roads have led to further agricultural expansion at the expense of forest trees. According to older residents of the Pacific coast, many large old ceibas were lost when the new coastal highway was built. The Petén, the largest area of rainforest left, is seeing rapid development. Wild-growing trees are an important aspect of the ceiba's image. The tall trees left in agricultural fields and those that have grown up on the ruins, as they have at Quiriguá and Copán, lend an air of mystery as well as a connection to the past. Tour guides bringing visitors to the lowlands often point them out and speak of the tree's sacredness to the Maya (especially since the development of La Ruta Maya).

LIVE OAK

The live oak's story shows how quickly a tree can become a valued cultural symbol and how multifaceted such a symbol can be. In the last 150 years, this Louisiana native, once limited to restricted habitats along waterways, has spread throughout the state and has become the premier shade tree, celebrated in poetry, paintings, and stories. Individual trees are valued at $30,000 or more for insurance purposes, sometimes as much as the home on the property. Tourist brochures imply the state is lined with allées leading to fantastic mansions, interspersed with quaint Cajun bayou scenes. In fact, the association with Southern plantation culture is so strong that other roles are often overlooked. Nevertheless, like the ceiba, the live oak has a number of distinct identities.

Native Americans and Live Oaks

Although written evidence is scarce, the live oak, like the ceiba, was a forest tree probably valued for practical reasons by American Indians of the region. The earliest settlements in Louisiana are on the coastal cheniers and salt domes called the "Five Islands": Jefferson, Avery, Weeks, Cote Blanche, and Belle Isle. These dry hills, once covered in live oak forests, offered homes with easy access to marsh habitats filled with abundant wild game and other foods. Inland, pre-historic inhabitants chose natural levees along the plentiful water-ways, as they did throughout the Southeast. By 5000 B.C. they had developed a hunting and gathering complex in the woodlands that covered much of the state. Although corn was introduced to the region before the arrival of Europeans, and farming was common on the rich soils of the natural levees, most American Indians relied on a combination of farming and hunting and gathering, following the seasonal harvests of both wild and cultivated plants. The forests were full of nut-bearing trees, among them hickory, pecan, and live oak. Even today, the sites of former settlements are extraordinarily rich in ethnobotanically important species.[23]

Acorns are a highly nutritious food, containing large amounts of protein, carbohydrates, and fat. Before the introduction of corn, acorns were probably a staple in the American Southeast. Along the Gulf and Atlantic coasts, live oak acorns were preferred for some uses because they are sweet, and thus do not require leaching to remove bitter tannins. They were ground into acorn meal and used to thicken venison soups, and they were roasted in hot embers like chestnuts. Their oil was used for cooking hominy and rice. John Lawson, on his trip to the Carolinas in the early 1700s, observed,

"The acorns thereof are as sweet as Chesnuts [sic], and the Indians draw an Oil from them, as sweet as that from the Olive, tho' of an Amber-Colour. With these Nuts, or Acorns, some have counterfeited the Cocoa, whereof they have made Chocolate, not to be distinguish'd by a good Palate . . . The Acorns make very fine pork."[24]

Carbonized *Quercus* remains have been found in archeological sites in Louisiana, but identification to species is not possible, so it is hard to know just how important live oak acorns might have been for food. The acorns do not store well; they either sprout quickly or are eaten by weevils. Brian Duhe, who participates in reenactments of colonial lifeways, told me of experiments he has conducted to find out how much time and energy it takes to prepare the acorns as food. He concluded that processing is so tedious and time-consuming that, given how much wild game is available year-round in Louisiana, live oak acorns were probably a supplemental seasonal food, gathered and eaten fresh, not a staple.

The trees had other practical uses. The bark and roots supply a red dye, and while the wood is so hard that it is difficult to work (especially without metal tools), it was a favorite for fires because it burns very hot. Live oaks also have an indirect role in subsistence: they attract a wide variety of game when the acorn crop comes in. Bear, deer, turkey, waterfowl, and many other species eat the acorns in great numbers each fall. Before they became extinct, passenger pigeons, another favorite food, would arrive in enormous numbers to gorge themselves on acorns of all kinds, including those of live oak.[25]

Another "product" of the live oak is Spanish moss (*Tillandsia*). The Natchez used it as a remedy in a sweat bath, packed it around babies on cradle boards as bedding and absorbent, and used it to fill pillows; others used it for menstrual pads, for plastering dwellings, and to make clothing.[26]

Managing or protecting live oaks might well have been part of subsistence strategies in what is now the southern United States. Further west, in what is now California, acorns were a major staple, and management of oak woodlands was and is a highly refined process. Periodic fires maintain stands of preferred oak species and destroy pests that otherwise eat the crop. When harvesters knock acorns off with sticks, they prune branches and stimulate lateral growth, which results in larger crops the following year. Southeastern peoples also used fire extensively to manage their environment. Areas around their villages were often open and park-like because of seasonal burning, and mast-bearing trees were abundant nearby. Although considered fire sensitive, live oaks can withstand quick fires used to clear underbrush and could have benefited from such management.[27]

Deliberate planting is another possibility. Lawson, in his description of live oaks in Carolina around 1700, notes, "I knew of two Trees of this Wood among the Indians, which were planted from the Acorn, and grew in the Freshes, and never saw any thing more beautiful of that kind. They are of an indifferent quick growth; of which there are two sorts." It is not clear from this if planting oaks was common practice, nor have I found other direct references to tree planting. But the trees are easy to transplant, and American Indians were skilled horticulturists, so it was well within their capabilities to plant either acorns or trees. His comment about "two sorts" is also intriguing. Was he referring to different species, perhaps one of the smaller coastal species, or were there cultivated varieties with different characteristics? Could this be a remnant of pre-corn management of trees?[28]

Grand Isle, at the mouth of Barataria Bay, is a young island, probably formed in the fourteenth century. It shows no evidence of having been settled permanently before 1700. Frederick Stielow, in his history of the island, says that "the growth of oaks was crucial for settlement for it gave the island an identity as an inhabitable plot of land in the midst of miles of treeless marshland." Scrub oaks became noticeable about 1770, and Stielow suggests that Amerindian groups, who stopped there frequently on hunting and fishing trips, may have "inadvertently dropped a portion of their acorn food-stuffs on such expeditions." Such dispersal would only be possible over short distances because of how quickly acorns sprout once they mature. They may also have planted them on purpose.[29]

There are good reasons to live near live oaks: they provide abundant shade, protection from high winds and rains, and convenient, safe places to hang valued items. In Florida, live oaks were part of typical settlements on the shores of Lake George: "As I passed along, I observed some elderly people reclined on skins spread on the ground, under the cool shade of spreading Oaks and Palms, that were ranged in front of their houses." In Louisiana, the Choctaws, who lived in the oak-pine forests north of Lake Pontchartrain in the nineteenth century, settled around large live oaks.[30]

There is no convincing evidence that the live oak was a sacred tree among Louisiana's native inhabitants, as the ceiba was among the Maya. A live oak in Youngsville is said to be sacred to the Chitimacha Indians, but no Chitimacha has confirmed this. I had conversations with a number of Chitimacha and Houma Indians who attended crafts festivals in the state, including several elders, and not one had any stories, legends, or other suggestions that live oaks had any special significance. (In neighboring Texas, however, the well-known Treaty Oak is said to have been sacred to native inhabitants.) A species that has been identified as sacred to some groups is the bald cypress, *Taxodium distichum*. Nearly all the truly old cypresses, which can reach one thousand years in age, have been felled for lumber. Younger specimens draped in moss and surrounded by fantastic emergent roots are still impressive, especially from a canoe.[31]

Live oaks and people have long influenced each other, however. Both seek the high spots within Louisiana's watery landscape. Any open, disturbed habitat created by shifting agriculture provided exactly the conditions live oaks need to get started; local squirrels and jays would take care of the planting. Humans created other new habitats that proved perfect for live oaks. Throughout the marshes are large mounds of shell middens, up to twenty feet deep, built up by generations of Indians subsisting on shellfish. Often these mounds were used for burials. Live oaks found them ideal habitat where they could perch with relatively dry feet. Although many of those mounds have been submerged by rising sea levels and covered by alluvial material, archeologists can spot them even today by the rows or clumps of live oaks that take advantage of this habitat raised slightly above the soggy plains.[32]

Live Oaking for Ships

The first Europeans to encounter live oaks recognized *Quercus virginiana* immediately as an oak, a genus that has a long history as both useful and sacred in the Old World. Colonizers and explorers were looking for natural resources, and what they saw was a great new source of timber. Cabeza de Vaca in his 1527 journey from what is now Tampa Bay to Tallahassee, noted the many *encinas* in Florida. He was using a word for the evergreen oaks of Spain (*Quercus ilex*, or Holm oak), recognizing the similarity to the trees of his homeland (where deciduous oaks are called *roble*). Encina continues to be part of many place names in the former Spanish holdings of North America. By the early 1600s, the English, too, had discovered extensive stands of the giant oaks along the Atlantic coast and on offshore islands. England has only deciduous oaks, so this new oak was christened "live," to emphasize its year-round growth habit. The French called it chêne vert, the green oak, also referring to its evergreen habit. Many places and families of Cajun descent bear the name Chenevert today.

It took enormous quantities of wood to maintain the great fleets of sailing ships on which colonial power depended. Oak had long been prized as superior for this purpose and the once vast stands of Europe were being rapidly depleted. Live oak wood proved to be superior to the best European oak for ship construction. It was harder by far than any other oak, yet also flexible. The curved and angled branches, and roots where they join the main trunk provided exceptionally strong pieces for sterns, transoms, futtocks, breasthooks, hanging knees, braces, and other parts needed for framing sailing ships. By the time of the Revolutionary War, it was widely recognized that the best American ships were made with live oak timbers. Demand for the wood was high both at home and abroad; during a period of "oak mania" in the early 1800s, many of the Atlantic coastal stands were cut.[33]

To ensure a supply for the navy, the new United States government began to set aside reserves of live oak stands. Louisiana was known to have live oaks. Father Pierre Charlevoix, writing about Barataria Bay in 1720, noted that the "finest oaks in the world might be cut there, the whole coast being covered by them." Bellin, a French cartographer, showed on his 1764 map of Louisiana a "forest of green oaks which are proper for construction" in that same area.[34] In the mid-1770s live oak was being cut on English lands along the Pearl River and sent (illegally) to the Spanish in New Orleans, where it was used to construct Spanish ships. The oak-rich lands of the Atchafalaya further west were less accessible; when Cathcart and Landreth were sent to survey Louisiana for live oak and cedar timbers in 1828–29 for the U.S. Navy (see Chapter 3), the only place they found oak being cut for timber was in Morgan City. Their survey resulted in 7,692 hectares (19,000 acres) being set aside for exclusive use by the navy. That didn't keep out poachers. In 1837, two hundred private vessels carrying timber worth about $1 million left the Atchafalaya. Three fourths of it was probably taken from the reserved government lands. In the winter of 1840–41 more was cut, much of it sold to the navy that already owned it.[35]

One plan to ensure the country's future oak supply called for the establishment of a live oak plantation. Managing woodlands with trees coppiced, pollarded, and trained to produce desired shapes was an ancient tradition in England as well as France. In the 1820s, Henry Marie Brackenridge, district judge for West Florida and sometime botanist, made a thorough study of live oaks and how they grew. He offered the results of his studies to President John Quincy Adams, recommending the establishment of a live oak plantation. With the president's enthusiastic backing, he began cultivating thousands of live oaks on Santa Rosa Island, near Pensacola, on his own land, which he donated for the cause.[36]

The navy never logged the reserved Louisiana live oak lands. When the United States acquired Florida from Spain in 1803, live oak became available closer to existing shipyards in the East. Then, demand for the wood dropped drastically with the introduction of steam-powered, steel-hulled ships. The plantation still exists, now known as the Naval Live Oaks Park of the Gulf Islands National Seashore. The dense stand of contorted, relatively small oaks hung with moss gives a sense of what the natural stands of coastal oaks in this area were probably like. Excellent educational displays show some of the life-sized wooden forms for ship parts, which used to be carried into the forest to help locate trees to cut.

Most people have forgotten this era of live oak mania. Occasionally, there are reminders. In 1992 Hurricane Andrew felled a large oak in Mobile, Alabama. The lumber was recruited by the U.S. Navy to repair the USS Constitution, called "Old Ironsides" for its durable hull, made of live oak timber. On a trip to Boston Harbor to visit the ship some years later, I recognized the unmistakable bark of a live oak among the stacked timbers nearby.

Oak Allées

The famous oak allées on the Mississippi River, part of the timeless image of gracious Southern life, are actually the lasting legacy of a small but powerful minority of Louisianans. The original plantation owners would probably be surprised to see the rows of enormous trees as they exist now, which often dwarf the fine mansions they were meant to showcase.

The landscape on which these carefully arranged trees were planted had already seen major changes by the mid-nineteenth century. Soon after the founding of New Orleans by the French in 1719, the first wave of European settlers arrived. Several thousand farmers, many from Germany, were lured by the extravagant claims made by John Law's Company of the Indies about the idyllic conditions in Louisiana, a paradise where anything would grow. They were given plots of land below New Orleans, along the Mississippi River. The great tangled mass of subtropical forest seemed threatening to many from Europe, where most old-growth forest had disappeared long ago. Whenever possible, they chose land that had already been farmed by American Indians; other settlers cleared the natural levees, home of the live oaks, as fast as they could, replacing them with food and export crops.

By mid-century a lot of the best land along the Mississippi had been claimed and was devoid of trees. In 1803, a traveler along the lower Mississippi was aghast at the barrenness of the landscape, without even a tree left as shelter in fields. Only occasional live oaks survived, either because they were too large to cut or because they served as witness trees, marking the boundaries of land holdings.[37]

That was about to change. Louisiana was transferred to the United States in 1803 and became a state in 1812. Wealthy Americans and French moved in and began to buy up smaller farms along the river to create huge holdings on which to grow sugar and cotton for export. They designed their plantations on an efficient, rectangular plan that emphasized straight lines: rows of crops and slave cabins, with the sugar refinery in one area, luxurious mansion and gardens for the owner in another. For planting designs they looked to Europe. On trips to the continent wealthy planters often visited Versailles and other formal gardens around grand country estates. A frequent element of these gardens was the allée—alley, or avenue—a double row of trees along walks and drives that provides both visual focus and shaded areas for travel. The formal style fit well with the classic Greek Revival mansions they were building, and suited their aristocratic pretensions.

In choosing live oaks for their allées, Americans were responding to another European preference. Oaks have a long history as the premier useful and sacred tree in much of Europe. Within the great oak forests that once covered much of the continent, ancient peoples used the wood, subsisted on acorns, worshipped in their shade, and buried their dead in hollow oak logs. Sacred fires of oak were kept burning year-round, and the trees were believed to be the home of Zeus and other gods. Words for oak were among the first words in the Proto-Indo European language. Sayings like "strong as an oak" are still common in English and other modern languages today. Their importance for ship timber was so crucial during the colonial era that the British spoke about the country's "Heart of Oak." In both England and France, concerns about the supply of oaks had led to legal protection of these trees. Landowners had long been urged to show their patriotic spirit by planting oaks; and their picturesque forms and longevity were widely praised by landscape artists.[38]

Some settlers of English background on the Atlantic coast of North America immediately saw the potential of live oaks as ornamentals. Even as shipbuilders were busily cutting the trees to use their wood or to make room for cotton, a few gentlemen in Georgia were letting live oaks mature on their island estates. Henry Brackenridge reported in 1828 that he had never seen a tree that improved so quickly in cultivation. In the South Carolina low country, planting of live oak allées began sometime in the 1700s. In the mid-nineteenth century, when John Muir walked through South Carolina on his way to Florida, he spent several days camped out in Bonaventure cemetery among giant live oaks that were 150 feet high and three or four feet in diameter. Duly impressed, he called the live oak the "most magnificent planted tree I have ever seen." In Savanna, Georgia, live oaks were planted early, too; by 1867, there were old trees already well established, giving the city well-shaded roads and parks like those in elegant European cities.[39]

Tradition has it that the oldest allée of oaks in Louisiana is at Oak Alley Plantation, in Vacherie. It is said these oaks were more than one hundred years old in 1836, when the plantation home was built, presumably planted by the previous owner of the property, an unidentified Frenchman. The plantation home's original name was Bon Séjour. It was changed because travelers on the Mississippi began to refer to it as Oak Alley, for the prominent double row of large trees, easily recognizable at a distance in the otherwise treeless landscape. A different theory holds that American Indian inhabitants of that site had planted the live oaks; another suggestion, from several people interviewed, was that settlers from the Carolinas brought the custom, along with actual live oak trees, to plant.

However it started, the fashion spread quickly during the peak of the plantation era from 1820 to 1865. Soon the River Road was lined with fantastic mansions and their new oak allées. The allée was a formal area of the property, an entrance to prepare for arrival at the mansion. As the trees matured, they provided welcome shade. Gardens for sitting or other activities were more likely to be toward the side or rear of the home. Martha Turnbull's forty years of diaries, kept at Rosedown Plantation in St. Francisville, give some other hints about the role of allées in everyday life. She called the double row of live oaks leading to her home "the Avenue." Each spring she noted when it was time to "hawl out the leaves," and mentioned who had done it. She also wrote of trimming the trees. She was surprised that her roses did not thrive for long under the live oaks; the trees grew much faster than she had imagined they would. Their rapid growth probably surprised many early planters. In this warm, humid region, especially when given ideal conditions of sunlight and freedom from competition, live oaks grow much faster than any European oaks, which often take one hundred years to reach an impressive size.[40]

The fashion of planting allées extended up river, and along the Red River, reaching at least as far north as Alexandria, well beyond what is considered the natural range of live oak. The region known as the Felicianas, just south of the border with Mississippi, was settled in the late 1700s by English-speaking immigrants from the Carolinas. There the influence was more in the English romantic tradition. Amid the rolling hills, allées took twists and turns, like the half-mile allée at Afton Villa in St. Francisville. Other plantation owners chose to put in large groves instead, clearing whole hillsides of native vegetation and replacing it with forests of live oaks as at Greenwood and Ambrosia Plantations. Some placed two specimen trees in front or lined their boundaries with live oaks.

But the popular image of antebellum homes, with moss-draped giant trees, is a romanticized reimaging of the past. Suzanne Turner, landscape historian at Louisiana State University, pointed out that in the mid-nineteenth century most of the allée trees would have been small—and possibly intended to stay that way. Plantation portraits of the era show that the focus was on the stately homes. Trees were decorative, leading the eye to the building. She believes that given the formal style of the plantations and the French influence on this region, planters very likely pruned the trees to keep them in bounds. Spanish moss was often removed because of its messy look, and the trees treated to prevent its coming back. While romantic landscape styles, with trees and shrubs closely encircling the house, were popular in the North, southerners preferred to keep plants away from their home and well controlled. A major concern was to keep circulation free around the home to prevent diseases.[41]

Today's stately allées owe their form largely to changes wrought by the Civil War (still referred to as The War by some). After the war, many plantations were abandoned. The live oaks were left free to grow as they pleased, in an ideal situation with plenty of light. They soon overtopped the decaying mansions and formed impressive allées and groves of giant trees. Others colonized abandoned agricultural areas. Legends developed about the trees, many of which became historical markers, like the Randall Oak in New Roads. Stories of valuables hidden in oaks to keep them from the Yankees are common, as are tales of cannonballs that date to Civil War battles.

By the early decades of the twentieth century, live oaks planted along the Mississippi River and bayous like the Teche and the Lafourche were becoming mature trees. Huge, draped in moss, they added romance to the ruined plantations that were beginning to attract tourists. When the annual "pilgrimages" or tours of old plantations began, the live oaks played a feature role. The 1941 *Guide to Louisiana* frequently points out the stately, ancient oaks at plantations along the various suggested travel routes and recommends picnics under clumps marking sites of former homes. The trees were magnificent specimens, the largest plants by far in the flat landscape, often dominating the local scene.

Travelers along the Mississippi today have the odd experience of seeing these old plantations alternating with enormous oil refineries. Starting earlier this century, the refineries began to buy up old plantation properties to extract the underlying oil and gas. Many of the old trees were removed or succumbed to pollution or root damage,

4.5 Historic oaks on private property can pose a challenge for public access. This one in New Roads is a Civil War memorial: William Randall is said to have written "Maryland, my Maryland" beneath its branches.

but a few of the new owners were persuaded to preserve the old allées. Some have planted live oaks at the entrances to their refineries and in enclosed outdoor picnic areas for their employees. If this is an attempt to blend in, to become a legitimate part of this landscape, it has mixed results. Even a large live oak is dwarfed by the enormous cylindrical tanks used to store petroleum, and appears relatively insignificant next to the elaborate system of pipes and stacks of the refineries. Longevity of these trees is also questionable, given the nature of exhaust from stacks.

The continued health of live oaks is of major concern in the state. As the trees age they are beginning to show the cumulative result of damage from lightning, hurricanes, and root damage. Keeping them in shape is costly, and replacing dying trees difficult since young trees put among the older ones are so shaded they cannot hope to catch up in size. Because the allées were planted in a relatively concentrated time span, they are aging all at once; in the next twenty-five years, many will be two hundred years old. Hurricane Andrew took out quite a few branches at several famous allées, leaving canopies thinned and owners worried about their future.

Meanwhile, another version of oak mania has hit Louisiana. Images of plantations have inspired homeowners to want live oaks on their properties all over the state, often to the despair of landscape designers, who know perfectly well how much space these trees need. Sometimes allée-like effects result when a whole row of neighbors agree to plant live oaks in front of their homes. Several streets in Baton Rouge have such plantings from the 1930s that now completely cover the street, with homes tucked in behind them instead of at the end of the long double row. In some subdivisions, developers have chosen to line the streets with live oaks, which in forty years will completely alter the scene. Large property owners still plant long rows of live oaks along their entrance drives. The largest shopping complex in Baton Rouge, Cortana Mall, has lined its access roads with many live oaks, as have a number of hospitals, schools, churches, and parks.

The Lone Live Oak

Walt Whitman wrote,

> I saw in Louisiana a live-oak growing,
> All alone stood it, and the moss hung down from the branches.[42]

Whitman, who glimpsed a live oak from the train when leaving New Orleans, described it as "uttering joyous leaves of dark green." His famous poem helped create another enduring American image. Some of the old giants still survived along the natural levees of rivers and bayous when Whitman toured the area in 1860. They stood out dramatically in sugarcane fields, welcome shade for those toiling in the hot sun. The moss-draped giant standing alone in a field, looming out of swampy mists or protecting a humble farmhouse was a popular image portrayed by poets and artists in the South, but especially Louisiana. To the Romantic imagination, nature was full of symbolism for the human observer.

In his history of Louisiana painters, Estill Curtis Pennington gives credit to Joseph Rusling Meeker for "creating for the nation's public the haunting image of the single moss-hung oak." Inspired by Longfellow's epic *Evangeline*, Meeker painted a series of mythical scenes of Acadians in the Atchafalaya swamps. Graceful, protective live oaks dominate these romantic paintings. Other artists of the

4.6 Lone live oaks stand out in the flat landscapes of sugarcane fields.

"Bayou School" who used live oak images included Richard Clague, William Henry Buck, and Alexander John Drysdale. Drysdale developed a basic formula of bayou, water lilies, and live oak, inspired by scenes in New Orleans' City Park. According to Pennington, the live oak became "an enduring compositional convention in Louisiana painting, outlasting criticism, changing technique, and even the tides of taste. Finally it becomes the ultimate artistic parody, still hanging proudly for sale on the iron railing of Jackson Square."[43]

The ideal live oaks shown by these artists are generally large and moss-draped, with branches reaching toward the ground. They are single trees, whole worlds in themselves, symbols of nature suitable for contemplation. They speak of isolation, endurance, self-sufficiency, romance, and the harmony of nature. None refers to plantations; if any humans intrude they are Indians, wanderers in the swamp, or humble settlers, their homes nestled in the protective shelter of the tree.

In the twentieth century this image was used to promote the state's natural attractions, especially to those wanting to escape the tensions of modern life. In the late nineteenth century, *Harper's*

Monthly printed illustrations and detailed descriptions of the state's wildlife, which of course included the oaks. The *Jefferson Parish Yearly Review* of 1938 is filled with photos of large live oaks, draped in moss. One, showing a small house among large oaks, bears this caption: "Barataria. This section of southern Louisiana has long been famous for its dreamlike beauty. Huge, moss-draped oaks, the gentle murmur of the bayou and the warm, fragrant air all add to the atmosphere of drowsy peace."[44] Similar descriptions are used in contemporary tourist brochures, which generally include at least a branch of live oak, with the requisite tendril of Spanish moss, framing a bed-and-breakfast or other attraction. The lone oak also adorns signs for residential developments, and is the logo of choice for many banks, retirement communities, environmental organizations, and even dentists.

The lone live oak is, of all the images of the tree, the closest to an image of nature, a nature that is larger and longer-lived than humans. Yet the very trees admired are almost all in cultural settings—in front of plantation homes, in fields, among houses along the bayous. Humans have in fact created conditions that allow the trees to develop their full potential, conditions that were relatively scarce before the lands were cleared and live oaks put in places with minimal competition.

Evangeline Oak

The Evangeline Oak is the single most famous tree in Louisiana. Within the state, it is known as the most photographed tree in the world. More than fifty thousand people travel to St. Martinville from all over the world each year to see it, and it has been the site of reunions, pilgrimages, political campaigns, festivals, and weddings. One college geography textbook even says that the common name of *Quercus virginiana* is "Evangeline oak." More than anything, though, this is an example of how storytelling can call a place into being.

Evangeline, the epic poem written by Henry Wadsworth Longfellow, was inspired by the story of the Acadian exile in the 1700s. At the time it was first published, in 1847, the world did not know about the expulsion of thousands of French-speaking people from Nova Scotia by the English. Forced off the land they had farmed for several generations, thousands of them wandered the world for years, searching for a new home. Many died before they were offered land in southern Louisiana, along the bayous. Groups of survivors made their way to their new Acadia, where they established small, self-sufficient farming communities beginning in 1775. French continued as their main language. They formed a distinct, separate group with the state, living in linear settlements that often stretched for miles along the bayous. Eventually some expanded into the swamps of the Atchafalaya basin and into the prairies, adapting their lifestyles to conditions there. As a group, they became known as the Cajuns.

Longfellow's interest was in the early years, when they were rudely thrown out of their northern lands. He had heard a legend that intrigued him about two lovers separated during the expulsion, who searched for each other for years. On the basis of this he created Evangeline, a pure and faithful girl who came to Louisiana searching for her betrothed, Gabriel, who had arrived there earlier. She found the home of Basil the Blacksmith, Gabriel's father, on the banks of the Teche. Learning that Gabriel had just left for points north (having given up on finding Evangeline again), she decided to follow him. The rest of the poem describes years of fruitless searching until she, too, gives up and becomes a nun in Philadelphia. The lovers are briefly reunited when Gabriel, an old man, lies dying in the hospital where Evangeline cares for the sick.

Longfellow had never seen a live oak, nor had he visited Louisiana. His descriptions of the swamps are based on others' accounts and his own fertile imagination. In the poem, northern oaks play a symbolic role in the Acadians' lost homelands, suggesting strength and endurance. Oaks also show up in Louisiana, draped with Spanish moss. In one scene in the poem, the trees whisper to Evangeline to have patience in her quest.

The poem was an immediate success and Evangeline became an international heroine, the model of Victorian modesty and faithfulness. Interest was also roused about the Acadian exile, and people began to look into the history of that event and at the Cajuns in a new way. Meanwhile, the story was being retold in Louisiana, with slight modifications. One new version of the story toward the end of the nineteenth century described a meeting between Evangeline and Gabriel under a live oak on the banks of Bayou Teche. In "Acadian Reminiscences: The True Story of Evangeline," by Felix Voorhies, the heroine (now identified as a real person named Emmeline

Labiche) arrives in St. Martinville only to find that her lover has married another. In her grief she loses her mind and soon dies. The historian Carl Brasseaux traced the evolution of the Evangeline story in his book *In Search of Evangeline* (1988). My description follows his reconstruction of events about how the live oak called Evangeline came to be a symbol of the Cajun people (or at least some of them).

Around the turn of the century, the people of St. Martinville settled on a specific live oak in their town as the tragic meeting place. They named it the Evangeline Oak. The idea was to attract visitors to the site. In 1902, the town was horrified one morning to discover that some villain had hacked off the tree's branches during the night, ruining it. There was great consternation among residents at this shameful deed; one letter to the editor of *The Weekly Messenger* wondered why nobody had guarded the important "sacred" landmark.[45]

Fortunately, there were other live oaks in the vicinity and a new tree was soon named Evangeline. This one, however, was on private property. That became a problem as more visitors began to arrive, and by 1930 the town had chosen a third tree, the current Evangeline. A tree at the nearby Longfellow-Evangeline State Commemorative Area was named Gabriel. The previous Evangeline, a fine specimen, is still growing behind the brick building next to the park. Remnants of an old sidewalk lead to it.

Before 1920, St. Martinville was primarily a local attraction, drawing visitors from as far away as New Orleans. In the 1920s two film versions of the Evangeline story were made. After one of them, Dolores Del Rio, who played Evangeline, had a statue of the heroine made in her own image and donated it to the town. By the end of the decade, St. Martinville was a widely known tourist destination. In 1928 the French poet Paul Claudel made a "pilgrimage" to the oak to affirm the strong connection between France and Louisiana's Acadians. Huey Long campaigned at the live oak for the Cajun vote when he was running for governor that same year. During this period, the Acadians began to adopt Evangeline as their heroine, their own "Joan of Arc," as Carl Brasseaux says in his book. He describes how Evangeline girls began to make trips to Canada and how Louisiana Acadians were adopted into the international Acadian organization, which had previously shunned them.

Brasseaux points out, however, that it was primarily the white-collar, middle-class Cajuns who took up Evangeline. Among the blue-collar contingent, about 70 percent of the whole group, Evangeline is not held in high regard and in fact is often ridiculed. That mixed response is also true among the citizens of St. Martinville, as I learned from speaking with them. The town is not particularly Cajun. Most of the French speakers who settled there came from France to escape the revolution. At one time the town was called Little Paris.

An interesting fact that does not seem to trouble anyone is that the current Evangeline Oak almost certainly was not yet growing when the Cajuns arrived in the 1700s. Back in 1935, when a famous oak man, Edwin Stephens, was looking for hundred-year-old trees (determined by a seventeen-foot circumference), Evangeline didn't make it. That means it could not have been the setting for the famous reunion. Then again, there was no reunion, according to Longfellow.

Regardless of the "facts," the tree and the area around it have become a highly symbolic place, important to the local community's identity and economy. In addition, the live oak has become part of Cajun identity. For many years live oaks were a backdrop to life in the area, not something to make a fuss about. Along the Teche, homes and barns were often shaded by live oaks left when settlers cleared their small plots for farms. Those who moved into the Atchafalaya swamp sought out the dry ridges marked by oaks, and harvested the Spanish moss from the oaks and cypresses. Tons of cured and dried moss were exported from the region each year for stuffing mattresses and couches. In the open expanses of the prairies to the west, where Cajuns raised rice and cattle, they planted trees around their homes: chinaberry and catalpa for firewood and fence posts, and often a live oak or two. On the cheniers to the south, they lived among oaks, too, and their cattle grazed in the open savanna of live oak, prickly pear, and palmetto. It was only in the twentieth century, when they were becoming conscious of themselves as a people with a distinctive culture, a source of pride, that they settled on the tree as a symbol.[46]

Two twentieth-century Cajun artists have played an important part in this process: George Rodrigue and Floyd Sonnier. Rodrigue's paintings are the more dramatic, with large, black oaks forming the backdrop against which he paints human figures. He says the live oaks are the Cajun symbol of hope, even though in many paintings

4.7 *In St. Martinville, images of the Evangeline Oak decorate everything from municipal trucks to badges worn by rangers.*

they appear to be more brooding than hopeful. Sonnier's oaks, by contrast, are detailed, leafy, protective trees. Generally there is one sheltering the homestead, a reassuring, friendly presence. When I asked him why he had live oaks in so many of his images, he was surprised, then told me that he lived and slept under them, so why wouldn't he include them. Later, when an article on my work was published in the Baton Rouge newspaper, he sent a card to thank me for talking about live oaks, and described the many trees he had planted on his own property.[47]

There is pride associated with the oaks, and a feeling of history and of belonging in this place. The largely Cajun town of Breaux Bridge put the live oak and the crawfish in its town logo earlier in the century, and is highly conscious of its old oaks. New Cajun suburban homes are likely to have two live oaks in front. A Cajun dictionary for sale in tourist stores shows the live oak on its cover along with a crawfish. At the annual Festival Acadienne, held in the shade of live oaks in Lafayette, the live oak decorates handkerchiefs, paintings, and T-shirts.

Live Oaks at Sacred Places

In southern Louisiana live oaks often grow near churches and within cemeteries. This association has some indigenous precedents: burial grounds had to be on high ground, which were also a favorite place for oaks. However, oaks have a long history as sacred trees among European cultures, and some of this association has clearly been transferred to the live oak.

The ancient beliefs about the oak as the home of Zeus and other gods has already been mentioned. Early Christian missionaries in Europe opposed oak worship, often cutting down sacred trees and groves. Some "Christianized" the trees instead, building their chapels in the groves. Eventually oaks (and other trees) came to play an important part in the new religion. The Virgin Mary has appeared in oaks throughout Europe (and more recently in North America), and the species is often associated with pilgrimage sites and other sacred places in the landscape.[48]

Southern Louisiana was settled largely by European Catholics, who brought their oak traditions along. In the early years, before churches were built, they often celebrated Mass in the shade of live oaks. In the nineteenth century, Father Rouquette, known to the Choctaw as Chata Ima, often spoke to them in the shade of one of the enormous live oaks native to this area of oak and pine forest near Lake Pontchartrain. One of his poems described the live oak as the tree of life of the Choctaws. Several of his small chapels in the forest were under oak trees, and eventually legends grew up that he lived in a live oak; a book about him even included a sketch of his mythical dwelling. Today the tradition of outdoor Mass on special occasions continues in some parishes.[49]

Many Catholic and Episcopal churches built in the 1800s had live oaks planted near the building, usually either at the entrance in front or in a small grove behind, which have now been turned into places for contemplation (see Chapter 2). Several Catholic retreat centers, including Manresa, in Convent, and Our Lady of the Oaks Retreat House, in Grand Coteau, are known for their live oak allées. At the Academy of the Sacred Heart in Grand Coteau, the long allée was supposedly planted by a priest who wanted a shaded walk on his way to say Mass for the sisters each day (one wonders how long he planned to live). These allées have been made into places of prayer:

4.8 Our Lady of the Oak shrine in Maringouin was established by a priest from Spain.

Stations of the Cross, statues of saints, and benches encourage contemplation. Private homes, too, often have shrines under live oaks with statues of Mary or St. Francis.

The diffusion of European oak traditions is still going on. In the small town of Maringouin the Catholic church has a shrine known as Our Lady of the Oak. Standing within the branches of a live oak is a statue of Mary, painted blue and white, surrounded by stars. In front of the tree are a small wooden altar and several benches for kneeling. When I knocked on the rectory door to inquire about this shrine, Father Ibañez, a priest from Spain, greeted me. He traced the origins of this devotion to an apparition of Mary in an evergreen oak in Spain during the Middle Ages. A few years earlier, when he had been back to visit, he decided to bring this devotion to Mary to Louisiana and purchased the statue now in the live oak. Each year in May, the month of Mary, his parish celebrates Mass under the oak; young girls crown the Virgin and receive their first communion there.

Some of Louisiana's most beautiful and famous cemeteries, like that of Grace Episcopal Church in St. Francisville, were planted with live oaks in the mid-nineteenth century and are now shady and romantic places. Many smaller burial grounds also have their oaks, and cemetery names often reflect this association. Although part of the association of oaks and graves can be attributed to soil and water conditions, it also indicates the diffusion of European traditions of placing evergreens, symbols of everlasting life, at burial places.[50]

Live Oak Society

Dr. Edwin L. Stephens, president of the University of Southwestern Louisiana, began the most extraordinary campaign for live oaks, one that continues to have a major effect on live oaks in the landscape today. In 1934, he published an article entitled "I Saw in Louisiana a Live Oak Growing," recalling Whitman's poem. Stephens had been impressed for some years by the fine live oaks in his region. In fact, he believed *Quercus virginiana* had been misnamed, claiming of Virginia, "I don't believe she has ever had much to show in the way of live oaks . . . I have traveled in the Gulf coastal region quite extensively in the last few years, and I can confidently report that Louisiana has more and bigger and better live oaks than any other state I have visited." He went on:

To my mind the live oak is the noblest of all our trees, the most to be admired for its beauty, most to be praised for its strength, most to be respected for its majesty, dignity and grandeur, most to be cherished and venerated for its age and character, and most to be loved with gratitude for its benefi- cence of shade for all the generations of man dwelling within its vicinity.[51]

He proposed the formation of the Louisiana Live Oak Associa- tion, whose members would be trees at least a hundred years old. First among the centenarians he listed was the Locke Breaux oak, the largest tree he knew, measuring 10.7 m (35 ft.) in circumference, 22.8 m (75 ft.) tall, with a spread of 50.6 m (166 ft.) in 1932. It was in St. Charles Parish, on the banks of the Mississippi, four miles above Hahnville. He identified forty-five others that were at least 5.2 m (17 ft.) in circumference, the minimum, he believed, to qualify as a member. Each member was to be sponsored by a human "attorney" who would measure it, give it an official name, and make sure it sup- plied annual dues of twenty-five acorns to the society. These would be planted at Southwestern Institute farm, in Lafayette, to yield trees for distribution throughout the state. The largest trees would be officers, elected for life.

His announcement generated much interest throughout the South. Nobody had ever heard of a society in which the trees were official members, yet nobody seemed to object. They did, however, object to a society limited to Louisiana. Because of a general outcry from readers, he expanded the society to include the whole South. Once the society was officially begun, he initiated an annual "pil- grimage" to visit prominent members and induct new ones. The society achieved some notoriety and plenty of press coverage, and Stephens made it into the *Guinness Book of World Records*. After his death, the society was in limbo for a while, its records transferred to several organizations in turn, but since 1966 it has been run by the Federated Garden Clubs of Louisiana. In 1996 there were more than three thousand registered members (including the Junior League members, who must have at least an 8-ft. [2.4-m] girth. Since then, there has been a surge in new applicants. As of October 2002, the membership had grown to more than four thousand.

While the tree membership in the society is large, the human element has remained minimal, as Dr. Stephens intended. It is run by a volunteer, chosen by the president of the Federated Garden Clubs of Louisiana, who sends out membership forms and talks to various groups and the press as requested. Verlyn Bercegay, who was in charge during the time I was doing research, had a library of scrapbooks filled with articles and photos of the society's activities through the years. Recently the whole list of trees, including their names, location, and measurements, has been put online.[52]

One of Dr. Stephens' goals was to protect the live oaks, for he had already seen how highway changes and rapid development threatened the trees. He actively tried to save a fine grove of trees in Breaux Bridge known as Paradise Woods, a spot to which artists flocked to paint. He was unsuccessful in that, but membership in the Live Oak Society has been used to save registered trees from being cut. Although it confers absolutely no legal protection, official status as a member can arouse such public sympathy when a tree is threatened that compromises are often made. Such oaks are no longer anonymous; they have been named, singled out, and recorded by people who have a personal relationship with them. Throughout the state I have met people proud of these ties, reassured to know their trees are inscribed somewhere. Most are not marked; this is a landscape of significance known only to the initiates.

Some of the original society members have died of old age or other causes. The Locke Breaux so admired by Dr. Stephens became the property of the Hooker Chemical Company of New York when they bought the land on which it stood in 1964. The new owners announced they were going to cut the tree, which led to a vigorous and successful campaign to save the tree that included Louisiana's governor. But within a few years the ancient tree went into a decline (along with all the other trees on the property), and by 1967 the old president was officially declared dead. Its final revenge was that it proved almost impossible to remove; even dynamite failed to destroy the remaining hollow trunk.[53]

The search for a new president eventually ended with the appointment of the Seven Sisters Oak in Old Lewisburg (a decision Stephens might have objected to since the tree has multiple trunks, which he said disqualified a candidate for largest tree). The induction ceremony in 1966 was a major event that included live oak doubloons and speeches by the town mayor and governor's representative. Since then new vice presidents have also been chosen. First vice president is the Middleton Oak in Charleston, South Carolina (31-ft. girth); second is the Cathedral Oak in Lafayette, Louisiana (27 ft.); third is the Lagarde Oak in Luling, Louisiana, (29 ft.), and fourth is the Martha Washington Live Oak in Audubon Park, New Orleans (no measurement given on website). Although Dr. Stephens would be proud of Louisiana's representation among the officers, I can't help but wonder how he'd feel about the fact that the officers are not all the largest society members.

It was Dr. Stephens' strong affinity for live oaks that led to the formation of his society, but it succeeded and continues to flourish because he touched on feelings that are widespread among people throughout the live oak's range. He gave them a way to honor trees that evoke strong emotional responses. Naming individuals acknowledges a personal relationship; appointing people as guardians gives the trees someone able to speak for and defend them, like friends or family members. Although much of the early correspondence among the "attorneys" regarding rules and exceptions is tongue-in-cheek, beneath the humor is a real bond and sense of responsibility.

There is also an element of the privileged speaking to each other in protecting the chosen. Whitewashing was a major subject of numerous "legal" opinions discussing the suitability of several proposed new members in the early years. Apparently the custom of painting lower trunks was considered tacky at best and to be avoided in the society. The practice was out of style among the privileged; it was and is still done in parts of Louisiana, especially among those of Cajun descent. Live Oak Society rules specifically forbid whitewashing. (The tree in question in the correspondence was judged innocent since it had no say in the matter.) The current president of the society, the Seven Sisters Oak in Lewisville, is on private land, surrounded by a fence, accessible only through permission of the owners (who are generous with such requests). Meanwhile, many people in neighboring communities have no idea of its existence. A clerk at a local Mandeville store said he found out about it only when his daughter's class went there on a school trip. Other owners of big trees not enrolled in the society often told me they were afraid registration would be costly and, once identified, their tree would be subject to other people's decisions. They preferred to keep their trees to themselves.

4.9 *The aging Cathedral Oak in Lafayette, vice president of the Live Oak Society, before it was damaged by a 2002 hurricane.*

Pedigree matters in the South, and live oaks are no exception. Trees famous for their size or historic importance are often chosen as seed sources and are a source of pride for their owners. The Friendship Oak of Mississippi, for instance, was the source of hundreds of thousands of oak seedlings given away in 1973 for replanting after Hurricane Camille struck the gulf in 1969. At one time it was possible to buy seedlings of the Evangeline Oak. More recently, the American Forests Association has been selling seedlings of the Seven Sisters Oak. Purchasers receive a certificate vouching that this is a direct descendant of Louisiana's champion tree. At more than 38 feet in circumference and a limb spread of over 132 feet, it is recognized by the National Register of Big Trees as the largest live oak known.[54]

Home and Community

Throughout southern Louisiana, and into northern parts of the state, live oaks are a symbol of home. Styles of planting vary, as do the homes. Pairs of trees in front or behind, single trees, or whole rows or groves can shade anything from elaborate mansions to simple cabins or modern ranch-style dwellings. Even trailers are tucked into the shade of fine old trees. As one person remarked, "You don't have to have a stately home to have a stately oak." Large specimens left over from plantation days can end up among new developments as the old properties are divided, so that new homes find themselves with already ancient trees. When they build, homeowners try to place their homes in relation to existing trees, as if they had planned the whole thing years ago. Unwittingly they often kill the trees by disturbing old roots or compacting the soil.

Within towns and cities, the role of trees has changed since the mid-nineteenth century, when John Downing published a series of books promoting the planting of trees on city streets, on college campuses, and other public places. Louisiana was late in adopting this approach to beautification. In the 1870s, when Savanna, Georgia, was already lined with graceful oaks, New Orleans was sadly lacking in trees, except within private gardens.[55] Toward the end of the century, though, live oaks began to be planted in some of the centers of towns springing up along the new railroad route that ran across the state. During the 1920s and 1930s the fashion spread rap-

4.10 "You don't have to have a stately home to have a stately live oak."

idly. Steele Burden, who planted so many live oaks himself, pointed out that many of today's oak-shaded boulevards in New Orleans (like St. Charles) and Baton Rouge date to that period. Now, when people plant oaks, they often cannot explain why; it just seems right. They are responding to a variety of messages received consciously and unconsciously: romanticized images of the plantation era; childhood memories of live oaks at home or at play; current images of live oak–shaded homes and lanes in art, advertising, movies, and post-cards. One man told me he likes imagining the trees in fifty or one hundred years, and thinks about all the people then enjoying the shade, as he has enjoyed the shade of oaks.

Mature oaks are a source of pride to individuals and communi-ties. Contributing to this are the popularity of oaks as a symbol of the plantation era, the connection to individual and historic trees promoted by the Live Oak Society, their role in Cajun identity, and an attitude toward nature that has become protective and admiring. Trees once taken for granted have become something to promote and celebrate. In the process of identifying and caring for oaks, com-munities become aware of themselves as well. Some towns proud of their oaks are along the Teche—Breaux Bridge, St. Martinville, New

Iberia, Garden City, and Jeannerette among them. St. Francisville, where the live oaks are almost certainly introduced, the trees are an important element in the annual "Audubon Pilgrimage" and in the everyday lives of residents. In Port Allen, across the Mississippi River from Baton Rouge, there is even a Mardi Gras crewe named "Good Friends of the Oaks," which carries a banner with the live oak's image.

Within towns and cities, live oaks are not evenly distributed. Important places within the community like courthouse squares, the courthouse itself, and other public buildings frequently have live oaks, sometimes accompanied by other symbolic trees like magnolia (the state flower), crape myrtle, and cypress. In northern Louisiana, beyond the tree's native range, they become more and more limited to such places. Schools, from day care centers to colleges, are other likely places to find live oaks. Louisiana State University at Baton Rouge, and campuses in Lafayette, Hammond, and Thibodeaux, all have fine stands of live oaks, as do Tulane and Notre Dame in New Orleans and many other campuses throughout the state. They recall descriptions of the Greek Academy and its tree-lined walks.

Live oaks are more common in affluent neighborhoods of cities. Cultural preferences are cited for this difference, but there are clearly other factors at work. Large low-income housing projects seldom install live oaks (or any trees, for that matter). Anyone with a small lot typical of lower-income neighborhoods is likely to choose smaller plants, or ones that produce food. Upkeep of live oaks can get expensive, too. In North Baton Rouge, live oaks that once shaded a middle-class neighborhood were taken down when it became a low-income area. Several people involved in urban planning and a resident of the area explained that the utility company that had formerly maintained the trees no longer wanted to bother with them.

Louisiana parks are famous for their live oaks. Their changing role mirrors changing cultural values and lifestyles. In the 1870s, City Park in New Orleans was a swampy expanse of giant old trees. Friedrich Ratzel, a German geographer traveling in the United States, had only rude words for this area, which he considered undeserving of the name "park." Today this same place is celebrated for its live oaks, which predate the founding of the city. Thousands of additional trees were planted there during the twentieth century. A map available at the visitor's center in the park outlines several walking tours with stories about individual trees, many of which have been measured, named, and enrolled in the Live Oak Society. Under the Dueling Oaks, according to the map, "hot-blooded Creoles" decided matters of honor by shooting each other. The grove of 249 old live oaks, believed to be the largest stand of its kind left, represents a piece of primordial landscape enclosed within a modern city. All over the state, live oaks are growing up in other parks. Depending on attitudes toward trees a hundred years from now, they may become similar sacred groves.

Roads and Travel

Years ago, it made sense to plant trees along roads. They marked the route, indicated important intersections, and gave protection from sun or wind or rain. Occasional large trees were also convenient rest stops. As travel rates have increased and the number of cars has gone up, trees in Louisiana have become a liability. They can obscure the view, drop branches, or get in the way of tall trucks; as roads have been widened even the trunks have become a problem. The Old Spanish Highway Stephens so admired for its thousands of oaks has far fewer oaks today; route 190 west of Baton Rouge once had planted oaks that are now mostly gone. Lafayette streets keep losing oaks as they are widened. I have received several requests for help from enraged citizens wanting to know how they can stop this process. Yet some trees remain as landmarks; the Back Brusly Oak is one example (see Figure 3.4). Another old marker in New Roads, the Stonaker Oak, is losing ground; larger and larger trucks passing beneath a branch that once arched across the road have reduced that limb to a stump.

Natural Stands

Remnants of native oaks along natural bayou levees persist. Highland Road in Baton Rouge, a major travel route from long ago and now one of the main arteries into the city, has ancient trees believed to predate European settlement. Community members have been struggling to protect these trees from development for years. Far to the west, along sections of Bayou Teche, are fine old live oaks that have grown on their own; until relatively recently the area was sparsely settled and not extensively cleared. The trees' area is shrinking as more people want to build on the levee, which results in increasing soil compaction.

As the forests and other native habitats of Louisiana have decreased in number and extent, they have become more valued, and are now seen as needing protection. Most of the cheniers near the coast were cleared long ago, but attempts are under way to restore two of the natural stands: Little Pecan Island, overseen by the Nature Conservancy, and Holleyman Sanctuary, managed by the Audubon Society. At Holleyman, an interpretive sign outside the mosquito-infested, tangled low forest of live oak and hackberry explains to people what is going on here. A few trails lead into the trees, but other than that, it is to be left without human interference. This is a version of the live oak completely different from the familiar images of home, community, or historic trees. The trees are small and often lopsided, valued not for their individuality or relationship to humans but as guardians and members of a nature we do not fully understand.

In the Barataria swamp, at Jean Lafitte Park, live oaks grow on old shell heaps, and along a boardwalk that leads into the swamp. These trees, too, are not like the trees of settled regions, with their spreading crowns. They are taller, competing for light with other species of the forest, and often have contorted branches. They are closer to the wild-growing trees that Cathcart and Landreth observed in the early nineteenth century. As in the recovering cheniers, humans are not absent, but rather managing and observing.

COMPARISONS

Within the cultural landscape, live oaks and ceibas occupy some remarkably similar niches. Both are prominent at community centers and gathering places like plazas and parks. They are likely to be near buildings associated with political power like courthouses and municipal offices. Schools, from kindergartens to universities, often have ceibas or live oaks. Within their native ranges, both species are likely to be along roadsides, at intersections and scattered in pastures and agricultural fields. Both mark ruins and once-settled areas. Finally, both are found at churches, cemeteries, and other sacred places. Images of the trees are frequent in signs and logos and tend to be associated with food, rest, comfort, ethnic identity, and other positive values.

One of the most striking differences between the two trees is that the ceiba appears to be a public tree, most often a symbol of country or town, while the live oak functions as public or private tree. In Louisiana, the live oak is an important image of home, and the relationship with the tree is highly personal and informal: people name the trees, enlist them in the Live Oak Society, and plant their own young trees in front of their new suburban homes. Another difference is that the ceiba is most often planted singly, while the live oak is frequently planted in large groups, in allées, boulevards, or groves. To some extent, this reflects their natural growth pattern in the wild. Yet there are also examples of ceibas lining roads, or forming groups in cemeteries or parks, just as there are single live oaks.

These distinct patterns reflect important cultural differences in land tenure, town structures, and architectural styles in Louisiana and Guatemala. In Louisiana, private property is common. A relatively small proportion of the population is involved in subsistence agriculture. Landscaping styles in towns often emphasize shade trees on streets and private lawns. Swings, tree houses, and other ways to get up into trees are a common sight. In Guatemala, by contrast, a high percentage of rural people raise food on small subsistence plots. Walls flank town and city streets, behind which are private houses and gardens. Huge trees like the ceiba are simply too big for most situations, and are reserved for plazas and other public spaces, along with private lands of the wealthy. An exception to this is in the rural lowlands, where single ceibas can be seen in fields, and young trees sprout prolifically.

Their paths to cultural prominence were different. European colonization has played a role in both regions, though the effects have been different. In Guatemala, the ceiba tree and its role as the tree of life for well over a thousand years gradually became incorporated as a part of the modern state. Throughout the Spanish Conquest, the Mayan people and their culture continued to be a vibrant presence. The current popular image of the ceiba in the plaza shows a blending of pre- and post-conquest images concerning the role of nature in culture. On the other hand, this cultural image, along with others, is being promoted by a political state, the result of the ceiba's adoption as the national tree. Knowledge of the tree is being taught through the school system, linked to a national identity intended to include a wide range of cultural groups.

The live oak's story shows how relatively quickly a tree species can come to characterize a region, and how many diverse meanings it can hold simultaneously. Much of the live oak's rise to prominence in the Louisiana landscape happened in the last 150 years. Europeans of French, English, Spanish, and other cultural background arrived in Louisiana with attitudes about oaks formed on the other side of the Atlantic. They transferred many of these to the live oak, from cutting the trees for timber to planting them in culturally important places. As in much of North America, the presence of earlier peoples and beliefs about trees has been largely ignored. But the live oak's character is different from that of Old World oaks, so the result has sometimes surprised everyone. New relationships have developed that reflect not only the people involved but also the nature of the trees. Unlike Guatemala, Louisiana has not officially adopted this tree as symbolic of the state. Live oaks resonate as an image of the American South that extends beyond state boundaries. Cajuns, though, have picked it up as one of their symbols. Notions about the species are transmitted from one generation to another through everyday landscapes, popular art, stories, and other informal means.

For both species, certain individuals have played especially important roles in this process. Two men were determined to make the ceiba Guatemala's national tree. If not for them, and the resolution passed in 1955, would the ceiba be planted so frequently in today's plazas? Would generations of children be learning to recognize this species and its connection to their country? In Louisiana, people like Steele Burden, who helped create today's shaded roads and campuses, have had a major effect on the landscape and all the people who live in and visit Baton Rouge. Edwin L. Stephens' Live Oak Society continues to play a role in the live oak's status as favored landscape species. Whitman's poem and Longfellow's story of Evangeline also had long-lasting consequences for the cultural attitudes toward live oaks.

Of course, being a member of a prominent species does not guarantee respect or protection for every individual tree. There are plenty of ceibas and live oaks in desperate situations due to crowding above and below ground. People often do not recognize or under-

4.11 Formal plantings of live oaks in front of the Baton Rouge courthouse contribute to the atmosphere of power.

stand them. Some believe that because of their great size they must be exceedingly strong, possibly immortal, and able to withstand anything. Others worry and fuss over them, knowing they are highly vulnerable within the cultural landscape. Young trees tend to be overlooked. Until they reach a particular size, they are just young trees (ceibas are more far more recognizable than live oaks when young), and not given special care or attention.

Almost all the highly celebrated trees of each species that I found were in cultural settings. While some are remnants of wild stands now surrounded by settlement, many were planted by people. Both trees have been spread well beyond their native range, the ceiba reaching higher elevations and the live oak moving north. The live oak has also moved into new niches within its native range. Because of their great adaptability, both species often survive in spite of challenges. In many situations they actually do better than in the wild, away from other trees that would normally compete for light and nutrients. These individuals mature into spectacular specimens, which humans then nurture and protect. Almost inevitably, such trees gather stories about them as generations of humans come and go.

Ceibas and live oaks were not inevitable choices for symbolic trees in Guatemala and Louisiana. How, where, and when they were chosen is the result of relationships that evolved through many individual choices, cultural values, biological realities of both humans and trees, and the response of trees to human activities. The relationships are still evolving. Their presence in culturally important places right now is part of their power in getting people to replicate the plantings, adding more and more in plazas of Guatemala and along drives and in front yards in Louisiana. In ten, twenty, or a hundred years, the situation of these trees will likely be different, as human values and ecological conditions continue to evolve.

Chapter 5

CODA

CHARISMATIC MEGAFLORA AND THE MAKING
OF LANDSCAPES

CEIBAS AND LIVE OAKS are examples of what one might call "charismatic megaflora."[1] Like their animal counterparts—whales and elephants—fully grown specimens capture the imagination and evoke awe among humans. Their sheer massiveness is mysterious. Bigger and older than humans, they can dwarf, and often outlast, built structures. They alter the microclimate in their vicinity and become whole ecosystems. Over the years they gather stories and legends about them. Even after they die they continue to inhabit the landscape, physically or, once their wood is removed, as memories. Much of their lives remains hidden, conducted in secret within their huge trunks, spreading canopy, and invisible root systems.

In the late twentieth century big trees became global icons of a nature no longer dominant but in need of protection. Unlike the megafauna, though, many of the largest and oldest trees grow in the midst of humanized landscapes, staying fixed in place for many human generations. People live out their lives in relation to them, so that the trees attain an almost immortal status, their origins lost far in the past. Deciphering each species' story is a fascinating excursion into cultural and natural history that must take into account ancient beliefs along with modern trends.

Essential to acknowledge is that trees are not passive backdrops for human activities, but active participants in the ongoing creation of places and landscapes, as well as personal and cultural identity. Like people, trees have qualities that help create their "personality" as human companions. Basic architecture, trunk shape and size, leaf and bark texture, and annual cycles vary tremendously from one species and one individual to another. Live oaks, with their low branches and sheltering form, invite intimacy; yet they can also be scary, harboring snakes, ghosts, or spirits within their dense, sometimes oppressive, shade. Tall ceibas, their huge buttresses splaying out in all directions from smooth fat trunks, appear more aloof, impersonal. Yet other ceibas offer generous shade and suggest a feeling of protection. Each individual tree has its own gestalt, a combination of its growth patterns and how humans work with and interpret it through its lifetime.

Over time, as trees acquire symbolic meanings, even their images have power. Like all good symbols, trees are multivocal, giving them depth and endurance in human societies. I quickly learned the folly of jumping to conclusions based on obvious symbolism. The live oaks of Louisiana, so closely tied to plantation culture, turn out to have a much more complex and varied significance to people living with them today. The "sacred tree of the Maya" still has an aura of mystery, but its protection in modern Guatemala is often linked to its legal status as the national tree. Depending on where they grow and how they are presented to members of a society, these trees can become integral to notions of home, nationality, ruling powers, ethnic identity, or region.

What surprised me most during this study was the scale at which individuals, through planting trees, can set in motion the transformation of landscapes, and the effect this can have on generations of people. Steele Burden, the man who planted so many live oaks in Baton Rouge, lived to see such changes. Are people like this simply acting out a cultural preference, carrying out on a grand scale what people see as desirable? Or do they in fact help create preferences among those who experience the trees fully grown? There is a wonderful quirkiness to this, a chance for unexpected developments in the landscape. Suppose the first allées on the Mississippi had been created with tulip poplars? How many other classic landscapes and styles derive from individual decisions to plant particular trees?

Writers, artists, and storytellers also play a much larger role than I had suspected in creating significant treescapes. The story of how the Evangeline Oak in St. Martinville came to be a pilgrimage site may appear convoluted and based on non-facts, but it probably reflects how many such places have come to be. It in no way detracts from the

5.1 *Since it was planted in 1828, the ceiba in San Francisco Petén has become a dominant image in the town.*

reality of such places or their vital importance to human societies. That a live oak should be the focus for a romantic tale of the past involving love and death is not surprising, given the long history of oaks among people of European descent. A legend, a poet's imagination, and a town's desire to attract tourists helped give form to this site, and since then local artists and thousands of photographs taken by professionals and tourists have preserved and developed it for posterity. Paintings and drawings have also created particular moods and images of live oaks that have become firmly attached to this species. Stories, images, schoolbook lessons, and interpretations of the past have created distinct images of the ceiba in Guatemala, too. The village ceiba, with Palín as the ideal, is one of them.

Another surprise was the sense of awe and reverence expressed by so many people toward live oaks. It suggests to me that, contrary to popular wisdom, many people in the modern secular world retain a sense of the sacred in their everyday lives. Cemetery and memorial plantings; private shrines, statues of Mary, and Stations of the Cross placed in and under live oaks; the many trees at churches and retreat centers—all were one kind of evidence of this. Live oaks are also a favorite backdrop for weddings and wedding photographs, recalling the role of large, symbolic trees as emblems of fertility. For many, the spirituality associated with the trees is more private. People spoke of prayer made easy under the oaks, of creativity and peace in their shade. This kind of relationship helps explain the fierceness with which people defend threatened trees.

Planting live oaks and ceibas at locations where ideals of perfection and power play a role, like town centers, courthouses, schools, churches, and community meeting places, recalls the ancient image of the tree as *axis mundi*. These places are set aside from the ordinary to allow the breaking through of truth, wisdom, insight—all qualities associated with gifts of the gods, the greater-than-human. Like the customary yew plantings in English cemeteries, these ordinary customs of tree choice and location carry a sense of "rightness" that suggests many truly ancient and largely unconscious cultural beliefs live on in modern society.

People also use such symbolism to announce to each other which places in the landscape matter, and where power is concentrated. Large trees can mark the center of a place, like the ceiba in the plaza, or its periphery, entrance, or pathways, as seen with the live oak. However, because the trees change as they age, contemporary images may have little to do with the intentions of the past generations that planted them. Sometimes it is the trees that have taken over, become the important place, while the human-built structures have fallen to ruin or simply disappeared.

The issue of legal standing and protection of ceibas and live oaks points to some of the different ways trees achieve such favored status in society. Ceiba trees were at one time protected from cutting because of widespread social norms based on the belief that these were sacred trees, associated with great power. Harming them was dangerous. This belief persists among some groups, while others simply admire the trees and prefer to leave them alone. However, for many people within the modern state of Guatemala, the main consequence for harming a tree is legal trouble since the government has decreed it be protected. The live oak, by contrast, was once a utilitarian tree; cutting it was definitely permissible (except for trees set aside for governmental use). In recent years, though, many towns in Louisiana have begun grassroots efforts to protect the trees in their

5.2 Catholic retreat centers, churches, and communities often place Stations of the Cross among live oaks. This one is on Catahoula Road in St. Martinville.

communities. They have passed tree ordinances that prohibit the cutting of trees over a certain size, even if they are on private land. Somehow these trees have come into the public domain, forming a new kind of sacred forest that is off limits to private owners unless they have community approval.[2]

Deliberate acts of vandalism against valued trees, as happened with the original Evangeline Oak (as well as other live oaks in the South) are often described as "murder" or attempted murder. Those who decide to do this know full well what such trees mean to a community; their aim is to hurt people, not just the tree. A building can be reconstructed, but a tree, once killed, will never be replaced during that generation's life span.

Sweeping generalizations concerning cultural attitudes toward these big trees are pointless, I found. Each person brings to tree encounters a host of reactions based on biological, cultural, and personal factors. Not every member of a given cultural group has uniformly positive experiences with either ceibas or live oaks. There are many Guatemalans, for instance, who admire ceibas from a distance, but who have no emotional attachment to them. Others may know about the ceiba of Palín, but walk by other ceibas day after day without noticing them or recognizing their symbolic importance, and that includes Mayans. There are also those who consider big trees a nuisance, a source of danger, something inappropriate within a civilized environment. As the history of the live oak has shown in Louisiana, attitudes toward this species have changed considerably in the last three hundred years, both within and between different cultural groups. My experience during fieldwork indicated that attitudes toward the trees differed far more between individuals within a specific cultural group than they did between different groups.

One theme that kept reappearing was the important role trees played in children's lives. Childhood memories of trees are powerful. Adults almost without exception could recall important trees from their childhood, and reported their sadness when they found such trees had died or been cut many years later. Whether the associations were positive (most) or negative, the trees had made a big impression.

Recent studies on the role of nature in children's lives suggests that "wild" places, like vacant lots, watercourses, and big trees, play crucial roles in helping children develop morally, intellectually, and

5.3 A Guatemalan child is dwarfed by the massive roots of a huge village ceiba.

emotionally. They are refuges where they can explore, think, and work out their relationships with the nonhuman. Such early experiences are a foundation for later growth, creativity, and positive environmental attitudes. Studies of children with attention deficit disorder have shown that after being in a green environment, they function better. Unfortunately, the studies also indicate that chances for this kind of interaction have diminished drastically as more and more of the world becomes urban and suburban. Research in low-income urban areas, where green space is often absent, revealed that children and adolescents were worried about protecting trees and wanted more green places to play. Watching videos of green places, exotic or local, is nothing like exploring the environment with the whole body. And playing among small trees, no matter how much easier they are to care for in the city, is nothing like getting lost for hours among the branches of a fine old one.[3]

CHARISMATIC MEGAFLORA IN THE MODERN WORLD

Urban growth, with its focus on cars, has changed the role of trees in cities and along highways. Trees planted during the nineteenth century as part of the effort to make cities more livable have declined dramatically. Along with more recently planted trees, the older ones are contending with air pollution, new diseases, crowding above and below ground, and street widening. The average life span of city trees is remarkably low. Tree shade, once considered so important for moderating summer heat, has been seen as less crucial since the adoption of air-conditioning (although trees are once again gaining favor as a way of lowering energy costs). New developments and shopping malls tend to favor tidy, fast-growing, and smaller trees (if any) amid vast expanses of grass and pavement. Urban foresters, a relatively new brand of tree experts, are doing their best to consider tree plantings from a larger perspective, looking at issues of biological diversity and wildlife habitat in addition to amenities for humans.

Surprisingly, I found that many people—including some tree experts—don't realize just how vulnerable trees can be to human intervention. Again and again, I saw and heard about enormous live oak trees killed by construction work that disturbed their roots. Research has shown that roots spread far beyond the crown, yet homeowners and builders, and even some tree specialists, still believe that as long as you dig outside the drip line, the tree will be fine. In fact, big equipment compacts the soil, especially the upper layers so essential for root functioning. Often roots get buried under tons of new fill, which then smothers them. Above ground, city trees are often hacked mercilessly. That large live oaks, ceibas, and other species throughout the world manage to live surrounded by pavement seems remarkable. Dedicated tree researchers continue to learn just how delicate an old tree can be; even humans walking on their roots can prove fatal. Persuading the public of this is a major challenge, and barriers can be costly and offensive to people.

Control over who decides the fate of trees has changed in both city and country. The chief villains named as tree killers are usually highway planners, utility crews, and developers, outsiders who know little about what matters to local residents. By the time the trees are cut, it is too late for outraged neighbors to remedy the situation. Public response to this varies. Guatemalans in general seemed to feel powerless to prevent harm to ceibas or other trees. In Louisiana, neighborhood groups (at least in the more affluent areas) have at times blocked traffic, chained themselves to trees, written letters, and demanded meetings to protect their sylvan neighbors. Some people have even purchased extra lots with large live oaks to prevent a particular tree's destruction by developers.

Landscape architects, planners, foresters, and tree specialists play crucial roles in creating and preserving significant tree places. Working with local people, asking them about specific trees, takes time and an open mind. But in this era of globalization, when so many people feel powerless over their lives, attention to the local treescape could make a major difference. Lists of "plant materials" mean little to those who may or may not know the names of local trees. But they can easily identify which trees matter, which trees they love or which trees hold special memories. Standard, uniform trees ordered from faraway wholesalers may seem pleasing and sensible along streets. However, according to what people voiced during this study, they often prefer the occasional big tree, given plenty of space, accompanied perhaps by benches, completely defying all attempts to control and contain it. Those are the trees that invoke awe and bring some kind of comfort. Opportunities to engage with trees is also essential. Touching, sitting under, leaning against, caring for in some way—all these foster relationships that matter.

NATURE AND CULTURE

What does all this suggest regarding the question of nature and culture? Is the ceiba of Palín a cultural artifact? What about the remnant stand of mature live oaks at City Park in New Orleans? Would we class these as part of nature or culture? Like many trees all over the world, including the ginkgo, these trees are growing in close association with humans, perhaps surviving not in spite of, but because of, human intervention.

Within the language of human-plant relationships, there is no generally accepted term that describes these long-term interactions with big old trees. They are not domesticated in the usual sense that they have been genetically altered or selected. But neither are they truly wild or "natural," since many have been altered physically by humans and may go through their entire life cycle within the sphere of human control. In some ways, the interaction is reminiscent of pet keeping. Big old trees in the cultural landscape are often companions more than natural resources or crops. People and communities adopt individual specimens, either taking them in from the wild or choosing to live near an established tree; they treat it differently, modify it physically, and give it an adaptive advantage within the domestic setting. In return, they benefit from its shade, its association with home, and a sense of stability and positive self-image. They mourn hurt or dying trees as they would family members—and in some cases have been known to bury the remains. (I once received a call from a woman who wanted to know if there was a "humane" way to dispose of a deceased oak in her yard.)

One problem with the nature-culture dichotomy is lumping humans into one group, the rest of earth's inhabitants into another. As this study of two particular trees and their association with humans indicates, reality is much more fluid than that. Ceibas and live oaks are examples of species that are integral to certain cultures in specific times and places. They have been particularly important, the focus of much attention by humans. At times, they seem to cross over into the human category; the boundaries are definitely unclear in terms of people's perceptions. Each species with which we interact, whether tree, flower, garden vegetable, or weed, is in a particular relationship with people. Interactions with each are influenced in part by cultural values of a specific time and place. Beyond that are other factors, including personal history and basic biology (much of which we do not understand), either of which can override a cultural belief system.

"Mutualism" may be the best word available to characterize these relationships with charismatic trees (and many other species). It implies an interdependence between two species, each giving something of value to the other. Mutualism, like friendship, involves two active participants, rather than one who acts, and one who is acted upon. The best outcome for both is to continue the relationship indefinitely, through changes and difficult times. If we were to consider human relationships with other species from this point of view, rather than from the more common perspective of humans as in control or acting upon nature, it could drastically alter our understanding of ourselves as a species on earth. It would also sidestep the categories "nature" and "culture."

When you get right down to the level of experience, the contact is between and among individual beings within a larger community. What happens there is mystery and always potentially new. I believe that the reason so many people insist on having big old trees nearby, and mourn their passing (even when they cause problems to wires and pavement), is because of their "individuality." Unlike a row of Bradford pears or clonal honey locusts, each live oak or ceiba (or ficus or whatever big tree is the subject) is an individual, growing into a distinct shape. In the built environment of towns and cities, amid the hard, straight, predictable lines, these trees with their curves, textures, and freedom of form seem to satisfy some human desire. Perhaps it is a memory of a time when there was no rigid distinction between humans and the rest of creation.

CITY PARK, NEW ORLEANS

Saturday afternoons, the live oaks in City Park, New Orleans, are host to a wide range of visitors. People come to picnic, exercise, feed the birds, or simply relax in the shade. Brochures available at the visitor center point out that these trees are older than the city. Each tree has been named, measured, and enrolled in the Live Oak Society. One story claims that Iberville camped among the trees when he founded New Orleans in 1719, on the banks of Bayou St. John, the passage between the Mississippi River and Lake Pontchartrain. Occasionally a little sightseeing train goes by, giving people a tour of the park and a glimpse of specific live oaks with names that include Peggy Read, Dreyfous, John Philip Sousa II, Enrique Alferez, Suicide, and Almighty.

From November until early January, during the darkest time of year, millions of lights, in all colors, shapes, and patterns, hang from the trees, creating huge balls, stars, spiderwebs, and garlands. People drive along slowly to admire them, cars crowded bumper to bumper, adding headlights and taillights to the show. It is the modern-day equivalent of ancient midwinter rituals of light in the sacred grove, only this grove is in the heart of a huge city. The place the geogra-

5.4 City Park live oak as caretaker. For New Orleans children, the live oaks in City Park, among the biggest and oldest in the state, are vastly more engaging than any man-made playground.

pher Ratzel called a "miserable swamp" more than a hundred years ago, unfit to deserve the name "park," has become a place of recreation for city dwellers, a protected piece of nature centered on a grove of moss-draped big old trees.

Wandering out into City Park after a visit to the art museum one Saturday in spring, I found a group of children playing among the oldest live oaks. "They let you climb on the trees," one of the young boys told me as he rushed up the limb of the sprawling Walking Oak. He and his friends had been there for hours. This is a world to be explored with the whole body, as children have done from time immemorial. In the middle of one of the most crime-ridden cities in the country, this live oak is a safe haven, at least during daylight hours. No signs warn people away from the tree; no railings keep anyone back. It is like that ceiba in the Mayan heaven, taking care of the children.

APPENDIX

TREE SPECIES NOTED IN TEXT

Common name	Latin name
Apple	*Malus pumila* P. Mill
Amate	*Ficus* spp.
Baobab	*Adansonia digitata* L.
Balsa	*Ochroma* spp.
Beech, European	*Fagus sylvatica* L.
Beech, American	*Fagus grandiflora* Ehrh.
Black gum	*Nyssa sylvatica* Marsh.
Breadfruit	*Artocarpus altilis* (S. Parkinson) Fosberg
Catalpa	*Catalpa bignonioides* Walt.
Cedar of Lebanon	*Cedrus libani*
Ceiba	*Ceiba pentandra*
Chestnut, sweet or Spanish	*Castanea sativa* Mill.
Chestnut, American	*Castanea dentata* (Marsh.) Borkh.
Chinaberry	*Melia azederach* L.
Cottonwood	*Populus fremontii* S. Wats.
Cumaru	*Dipteryx odorata* (Aublet) Willd.
Cypress	*Cupressus*
Cypress, bald	*Taxodium distichum*
Cypress, Montezuma bald	*Taxodium mucronatum* Ten.
Durian	*Durio zibethinus* Murray
Elm, American	*Ulmus americana* L.
Elm, English	*Ulmus procera* Salis.
Eucalyptus	*Eucalyptus* spp.
Ginkgo	*Ginkgo biloba* L.
Hackberry (sugarberry)	*Celtis laevigata* Willd.
Kauri	*Agathis australis* (D. Don) Steudel

Linden	*Tilia* spp.
Magnolia, Southern	*Magnolia grandiflora* L.
Maple, sugar	*Acer saccharum* Marsh.
Monkey nut (castanha de macaco)	*Ariniana micrantha* Lecythis
zabucajo Aubl.	
Monkeypuzzle	*Araucaria araucana* (Molina) K. Koch
Oak, coast live	*Quercus agrifolia* Née
Oak, cork	*Quercus suber* L.
Oak, English	*Quercus robur* L.
Oak, Holm or holly	*Quercus ilex* L.
Oak, interior live	*Quercus wislizenii* A. DC
Oak, live or Southern live	*Quercus virginiana*
Olive	*Olea europaea* L.
Orange	*Citrus sinensis* (L.) Osbeck
Osage Orange	*Maclura pomifera* (Raf.) Schneid.
Pecan	*Carya illinoensis* (Wangenh.) K. Koch
Pine, bristlecone	*Pinus aristada* Englm.
Pine, loblolly	*Pinus taeda* L.
Pine, longleaf	*Pinus palustris* Mill.
Pine, slash	*Pinus eliottii* Englem.
Pochote (pochotl)	*Ceiba aesculifolia*
Poplar	*Populus* spp.
Red silk cotton tree	*Bombax malabaricum* DC
Redwood	*Sequoiadendron sempervirens* (Lamb. ex D. Don) Endl.
Redwood, dawn	*Metasequoia glyptostroboides* Hu & W. C. Cheng
Redwood, giant	*Sequoiadendron giganteum* (Lindl.) Buchh.
Sequoia, giant	*Sequoia gigantea* (Lindl.) Decne.
Totara	*Podocarpus totara* G. Bennett ex D. Don
Tulip poplar	*Liriodendron tulipifera* L.
Willow	*Salix* spp.
Yew	*Taxus baccata* L.

NOTES

NOTES FROM THE FIELD

CHAPTER ONE

1. Evelyn 1972 (1662); on tree marriage in India, Majupuria 1989 and Parkin chapter in Seeland 1997; legal standing for trees, Stone 1974; "ents," Tolkien 1973; ordaining trees as monks, Darlington 1998; descent from ceibas, Barrera Vasquez 1976.

2. See Friedrich 1970 on early tree words; Rival 1998 has excellent contemporary anthropological studies of trees in a variety of human societies.

3. Oak woodlands of Portugal and Spain, Parsons 1962; California woodlands, Blackburn and Anderson 1993; English woodlands, Rackham 1976; Mediterranean olive groves, Lewington and Parker 1999; cypress, Semple 1931; New England elms, Campanella 1999; management of wild plants, Anderson 1999.

4. English landscapes, Hoskins 1956; New England, Meinig 1979; elms, Clouston and Stansfield 1979, Richans 1983, Hoskins 1956; prairie plantings, Anderson 1957 and Sutton 1982; hedges in New Zealand, Price 1993.

5. Oranges, Gade 1976b; apples, Anderson 1984; eucalyptus, Dickinson 1969; ginkgo, Lewington and Parker 1999.

6. Mikesell 1969; Darby 1956; Schama 1995; Lewington and Parker 1999; Packenham 1997.

7. American Forests runs the Famous and Historic Tree Program and sells progeny of famous trees; a story in the *New York Times* by Robbins (2001) announced the supertree gene project; see other interesting books on this topic by Nicholson 1922 and Preston 1972.

8. Davies 1988 is an interesting essay on this topic by a geographer; Frazer 1966 (1922). Jung 1976:233–271 gives examples of tree symbols from different cultures and religious traditions.

9. Eliade 1969; for thorough treatment of bodhi tree see Simoons 1998; on sacred trees in India and Africa, see Majupuria 1989; Harlan, De Wet, and Stemler 1976; Gadgil and Vartak 1976. Sacred trees in general, Altman 1994. Note that there have been misinterpretations by Western scientists about so-called sacred trees and forests, especially in Africa. Critical discussion of specific examples are found in Seeland 1997.

10. Daniels 1988; Lawrence 1993.

11. Entrikin 1991; Richardson 1989; Richardson and Dunton 1989; von Maltzahn 1994; Meinig 1979. The work of geographer Yi-Fu Tuan has been important in my own work because he so often deals with the hidden dimensions of landscape and the importance of the physical body in experiencing the world. His writings on topophilia, pet-keeping, gardens, fear, and many other topics have had a profound influence in shaping the questions I have asked.

12. Kellert and Wilson 1993; Appleton 1975.

13. Lawrence 1988; Zube 1978; Arnold 1980; Jones and Rossman 1988; Downing 1991; Jackson 1952b.

14. Clay 1957–58; Stilgoe 1995; Kahn and Kellert 2002 has a variety of studies on this subject.

15. Richardson 1989.

16. Ethnography has been defined as "the work of describing culture" (Spradley 1980:3). It is conducted by observing, listening, analyzing, and recording. "Rather than *studying people*, ethnography means *learning from people*," says Spradley (1980:3), who goes on to say that ethnographers deal with three major topics: what people do (behavior), what they know (knowledge), and what they use (artifacts). In addition, Rapoport (1990:11) suggests that to understand how people react to their environment, the nonverbal communication approaches used in ethnology are the least used although they are the "simplest, most direct and most immediate" and lend themselves to easy interpretation and comparison with other studies.

17. See Gade 1999 for a good discussion of this.

CHAPTER TWO

1. Maynard 1963:91.

2. This business of suddenly dropping large limbs is not unusual. It often happens on still, sunny days, the result of a largely dead limb going through uneven heating, which can cause major stress. In Lewisburg, I heard the story of the Grandberry Oak, which dropped a limb the day Dr. Grandberry died, to everyone's amazement. See also Orso 1992:97.

3. Since this research was done, some of the plantations have added more interpretive material concerning the lives of slaves. Kathe Hambrick's museum has provided motivation, as has research done by a number of people at LSU and elsewhere.

CHAPTER THREE

1. See Baker 1965. For earlier suggestions about ceiba, see Zand 1941; Neal 1949; Bor 1953.

2. See Howe 1906 and Sauer 1971, also further discussion on ceiba names in Chapter 4.

3. Because of the long-standing difficulty of exact identification and its great variability, *Ceiba pentandra* (L.) Gaertn. has also been called *Bombax pentandrum*, *Eriodendron afractuosum*, and various other names.

4. Sanchez Vindas 1983:76; Pennington and Sarukhan 1960:290.

5. Standley and Steyermark 1949.

6. See Howe 1906 as well as discussion in Chapter 4 on cultural history.

7. Sapper 1897.

8. Zand 1941.

9. For descriptions of the flora of this region, see Lundell 1937.

10. Toledo 1976; for bats, Elmqvist et al. 1992; Murawski and Hamrick 1992.

11. Record and Hess 1943; Baker 1965.

12. Oviedo y Valdez quoted in Standley 1923:790.

13. For a listing see Gonzalez Ayala 1992.

14. The other species (and one variety) are *Q. geminate, Q. minima, Q. fusiformis, Q. brandegei, Q. oleoides, Q. oleoides* var. *sagraena.*

15. One reference to sweetness variation and olive oil in Harlow and Harrar 1958. Also, Malcolm Tucker, at the LSU Rural History Museum, told me in 1995 that he had tried to grow acorns from live oaks on Pecan Island, which are said to have larger, sweeter acorns.

16. For a discussion of plant communities in the coastal area see Platt and Schwartz 1990 and Greller 1990.

17. Craig et al. 1987.

18. Condrey 1995 describes some of the historical maps in the Hill Library at LSU.

19. Cathcart and Landreth quoted in Newton 1985:34.

20. Newton 1985:34.

21. Newton 1985:134.

22. Silver 1990; for a discussion of acorns as wildlife food source see Martin, Zim, and Nelson 1951.

23. Brackenridge 1980 (1828).

24. Stephens 1931.

CHAPTER FOUR

1. Standley and Steyermark 1949; Gonzalez Ayala 1992; Alcorn 1984.

2. Schele and Freidel 1990:66–67. Also see unpublished thesis by Guest 1995 on ceiba as sacred tree in the Yucatán.

3. Schele and Freidel 1990:85.

4. Carrasco 1990 has an illustration of children being fed by the ceiba; Aguilera 1985; Vega 1938. On ceibas as human ancestors, Barrera Vazquez 1976.

5. Villagutierre Soto-Mayor 1983.

6. Sahagún 1950:103.

7. Oviedo y Valdez quoted in Standley 1923:790.

8. Casteñada 1962 tells the full story.

9. Folan, Kintz, and Fletcher 1983.

10. Cortés y Larraz 1958; Sapper 1897.

11. Stoll 1886; Redfield 1936. Alcorn 1984 reports that among the Huastec the ceiba is still associated with water.

12. For the Beng, see Gottlieb 1992. For Jamaica, see Rashford 1985.

13. About the history and function of plazas, see Gade 1976a; Richardson 1978; Elbow 1975. Low 1993 shows that the plaza is not simply a Spanish introduction, as was long believed, but a melding of indigenous and introduced patterns.

14. Bernal Díaz del Castillo, *True History of the Conquest of Mexico,* quoted in Standley 1923.

15. Polonsky Celcer 1962.

16. Polonsky Celcer 1962. My translation.

17. Polonsky Celcer 1962.

18. For a description of the original ceiba in all its glory see Batres Jáuregui 1948 (1916).

19. Chinchilla Aguilar 1960.

20. Polonsky Celcer 1962.

21. Proyecto Guauhitemala had published two volumes on the country's trees by 1995, each covering twelve tree species. The books include full-page color photographs, scientific and common names, cultural traditions, full descriptions, propagation, uses, and some poetry.

22. In Boston, someone is in fact growing a ceiba in a container, inside. It can be done, but from the description, the tree is not exactly becoming a bonsai, since the owner reports having to hack it back. *Natural History* (November 1999).

23. Kniffen, Gregory, and Stokes 1987; Hudson 1976; Dunn 1983.

24. On food value of acorns see Smith 1987. Other uses in Hudson 1976 and Van Doren 1928. Quote from Lawson 1966 (1709):92–93.

25. The experiment on live oak acorns as food is described in Duhe 1980. Firewood use, Dunn 1983. Animals attracted to live oaks, Martin, Zim, and Nelson 1951; Schorger 1973.

26. See Kniffen 1979 and Swanton 1911.

27. California oak management in Blackburn and Anderson 1993. For Southeast see Silver 1990; Delcourt 1977; Platt and Schwartz 1990.

28. Lawson 1966 (1709).

29. Stielow 1975.

30. Quote from Van Doren 1928.

31. A photo and mention of the so-called Chitimacha tree is in Ethelyn Orso's fine book, *Louisiana Live Oak Lore* (1992). She had found no confirmation of its sacred status either. For notes on cypress as sacred tree, see Swanton 1911. In Texas, by contrast, it is believed that the famous Treaty Oak in Austin is the last remnant of a grove of oaks sacred to American Indians of that region, so there may well be more to be discovered on this topic.

32. Haag 1971.

33. I am indebted for most of this information to an excellent, lively book entitled *Live Oaking*, by Wood (1981). She pieced together the history of this era through historic documents, letters, and visual records. See also Saver 1971 for early Spanish explorers and live oak.

34. Condrey 1995. Dr. Condrey was kind enough to introduce me to some of the fine historic maps, at the time undocumented, in special collections in the Hill Library at LSU.

35. Wood 1981; Newton 1985.

36. On methods of shaping trees, see Rackham 1976 and Schama 1995. Brackenridge's 1828 letter was reproduced in 1980 and was made available to me at the library at the Pensacola Naval Station park.

37. Rykels 1991; Orso 1992.

38. Frazer 1966 (1922) has extensive listings of customs and religious beliefs surrounding many different trees. Much of it concerns oaks. See Friedrich 1970 for various words for oaks in different languages.

39. Dunbar's unpublished thesis (1991) is about live oaks in the Carolina low country. Muir 1981 contains a description of his time at Bonaventure cemetery. Ratzel 1988 describes Savannah in 1867.

40. Martha Turnbull's unpublished diaries (1855–1894) contain many interesting observations on gardening in the South during the time, including changes after the war. They are at the Hill Library at LSU.

41. Bonner 1977 is one of the few articles written on this topic. Conversations with

Suzanne Turner, who has specialized in historic gardens of Louisiana, were of great help.

42. Whitman 1931.

43. Pennington 1991:75, 77.

44. *Jefferson Parish Review* (1938).

45. An Acadian 1902.

46. For more on Cajuns and how they lived on the land, see Comeaux 1983; Post 1974; Kniffen 1979.

47. See Rodrigue 1976 for more in that artist's own words on live oaks and their meaning.

48. Nolan 1986 on pilgrimage sites; Glacken 1967 and Schama 1995 on attitudes toward oaks in Europe.

49. D'Antoni 1986 has drawings of chapels in oak.

50. Nakagawa 1987.

51. Stephens 1934:19. His papers and letters at Southwestern Louisiana State University in Lafayette contain much interesting information regarding the Live Oak Society, too.

52. To find the list, go to louisianagardenclubs.com, and follow links to the Live Oak Society.

53. Dysart 1968. The tree's demise was covered in quite a few articles in various newspapers.

54. See Haines 1973 on the Friendship Oak; for current listing of American Forests historic trees see www.historictrees.org.

55. Downing 1991 (1850); Ratzel 1988.

CHAPTER FIVE

1. My thanks to Liz Thompson, naturalist with the Nature Conservancy in Vermont, for this term.

2. According to the Live Oak Society webpage, the Louisiana Department of Transportation and Development has issued a new policy regarding "significant" trees growing along public roads. These trees will receive special consideration during highway and utility work. The definition of "significant" is instructive. It expresses clear cultural preferences for certain species, acknowledges the importance of individual trees to human communities, and insists that the trees be healthy:

> For the purposes of this policy, a significant tree is a live oak, red oak, white oak, magnolia or cypress that is considered aesthetically important, 18" or greater in diameter at breast height . . . and having a form that separates it from the surrounding vegetation or is considered historic. A historic tree is a tree that stands at a place where an event of historic significance occurred that had local, regional, or national importance. A tree may also be considered historic if it has taken on a legendary stature to the community; mentioned in literature or documents of historic value; considered unusual due to size, age or has landmark status. Significant trees must be in good health and not in a declining condition. (Revised regulations issued by Louisiana's Department of Transportation and Development on May 31, 2002 [EDSM No, I.1.1.21]. Accessed on the LOS webpage, April 4, 2003)

3. See Kahn and Kellert 2002 for a diverse collection of research on this topic.

REFERENCES

Agnew, John A., and James S. Duncan, eds.1989. The Power of Place: Bringing Together Geographical and Sociological Imagination. Boston: Unwin Hyman.

Aguilera, Carman. 1985.Flora y Fauna Mexicana: Mitología y Tradiciones. Mexico City: Editorial Everest Mexicana.

Alcorn, Janice B. 1984. Huastec Mayan Ethnobotany. Austin: University of Texas Press.

Altman, Nathaniel. 1994. Sacred Trees. San Francisco: Sierra Club Books.

An Acadian. 1902. Shockingly Mutilated. The Weekly Messenger, St. Martinville, January 4.

Anderson, Edgar. 1957. The Cornbelt Farmer and the Cornbelt Landscape. Landscape 6:3–4.

———. 1960. The Evolution of Domestication. In: Evolution after Darwin. Ed. Sol Tax, 67–84. Chicago: University of Chicago Press.

Anderson, Kat. 1999. The Fire, Pruning, and Coppice Management of Temperate Ecosystems for Basketry Material by California Indian Tribes. Human Ecology 27:1.

Anderson, Katharine [Kit]. 1984. Volunteer Apple Trees in Vermont. The Vermont Geographer 3.

Appel, D. N. 1986. Recognition of Oak Wilt in Live Oak. Journal of Arboriculture 12:213–218.

Appleton, Jay. 1975. The Experience of Landscape. London and New York: Wiley.

Arnold, Henry F.. 1980. Trees in Urban Design. New York: Van Nostrand Reinhold.

Arreola, Daniel. 1993. Plazas of San Diego Texas: Signatures of Mexican-American Place Identity. Places 8:80–86.

Baker, Herbert G. 1965. The Evolution of the Cultivated Kapok Tree: A Probable West African Product. In: Ecology and Economic Development in Tropical Africa. Ed. David Brokensha, 185–216. Berkeley: Institute of International Studies, University of California.

Barrera Vazquez, Alfredo. 1976. La Ceiba-Cocodrillo. *Anales, Instituto Nacional de Antropología e Historia* 5:187–208.

Batres Jáuregui, Antonio. 1948 (1916). La América Central ante la Historia. Guatemala: Casa Colorada, Marroquin Hnos. III.

Blackburn, Thomas C., and Kat Anderson, eds. 1993. Before the Wilderness: Environmental Management by Native Californians. Menlo Park, Calif.: Ballena Press.

Bonner, James C. 1977. House and Landscape Design in the Antebellum South. *Landscape* 2:2–8.

Bor, N. L. 1953. Manual of Indian Forest Botany. Oxford: Oxford University Press.

Brackenridge, H. M. 1980 (1828). Letter on the Culture of Live Oak. Pensacola: University of West Florida, John C. Pace Library. Library Publications No. 10.

Bragg, Rick. 1996. Termites Haunt, Topple, Mighty Oaks in Leafy New Orleans. The New York Times, p. 10.

Brasseaux, Carl A. 1988. In Search of Evangeline. Thibodeaux, La.: Blue Heron Press.

Campanella, Thomas J. 1999. Republic of Shade: The Emergence of the American Elm as a Cultural and Urban Design Element in Nineteenth-Century New England. Unpublished Ph.D. diss., Department of Urban Studies and Planning, Massachusetts Institute of Technology.

Carrasco, David. 1990. Religions of Mesoamerica: Cosmovision and Ceremonial Centers. New York: Harper and Row.

Casteñada, Gabriel Angel. 1962. La Pochota. In: Monografía Antológica del Árbol. Ed. Enrique Polonsky Celcer, 40–44. Guatemala: Centro Editorial "Jose de Pineda Ibarra."

Chawla, Louise. 2002. Spots of Time: Manifold Ways of Being in Nature in Childhood. In: Children and Nature: Psychological, Sociocultural and Evolutionary Investigations. Ed. Peter K. Kahn and Stephen Kellert, 199–225. Cambridge: MIT Press.

Chinchilla Aguilar, Ernesto. 1960. Historia y Tradiciones de la Ciudad de Amatitlán. Guatemala: Ministerio de Educación Pública.

Clay, Grady. 1957–1958. Remembered Landscapes. *Landscape* 7:7–9.

Clouston, Brian, and Kathy Stansfield, eds. 1979. After the Elm. London: William Hernemann Ltd.

Comeaux, Malcolm. 1983. Louisiana's Acadians: The Environmental Impact. In: The Cajuns: Essays on Their History and Culture. Ed. Glenn R. Conrad, 109–126. Lafayette: Center for Louisiana Studies, University of Southwestern Louisiana.

Condrey, Richard E. 1995. Discover Louisiana's Environmental Past: History Reveals Exotic Wildlife and Stunning Natural Landscapes. *Louisiana Environmentalist* 3:10–17.

Cornish, Vaughn. 1946. The Churchyard Yew and Immortality. London: Frederick Muller Ltd.

Cortés y Larraz, Pedro. 1958. Descripción Geográfica-Moral de la Diocesis de Goathemala. Guatemala: La Sociedad de Geografía e Historia de Guatemala.

Craig, Nancy Jo, Latimore M. Smith, Nelwyn M. Gilmore, Gary D. Lester, and Alanea M. Williams. 1987. The Natural Communities of Coastal Louisiana: Classification and Description. Baton Rouge: Louisiana Department of Wildlife and Fisheries.

Cullen, Ed. 1995. Down to Earth Oaks: Ph.D. Candidate Uncovers Tales of Grandeur and Goofiness While Studying the Live Oak. Baton Rouge Sunday Advocate, March 12.

Daniels, Stephen. 1988. The Political Iconography of Woodland in Later Georgian England. In: The Iconography of Landscape: Essays on the Symbolic Representation, Design and Use of Past Environments. Ed. Denis Cosgrove and Stephen Daniels. Cambridge: Cambridge University Press.

D'Antoni, Blaise C. 1986. Chahta-Ima and St. Tammany's Choctaws. *The St. Tammany Historical Society Gazette* 7:1–187.

Darby, H. C. 1956. The Clearing of the Woodlands in Europe. In: Man's Role in Changing the Face of the Earth. Ed. William L. Thomas Jr. 183–216. Chicago and London: University of Chicago Press.

Darlington, Susan M. 1998. The Ordination of a Tree: The Buddhist Ecology Movement in Thailand. *Ethnology* 37(1):1–15.

Davies, Douglas. 1988. The Evocative Symbolism of Trees. In: The Iconography of Landscape. Ed. D. Cosgrove and Stephen Daniels, 32–42. Cambridge: Cambridge University Press.

Delcourt, Hazel R., and Paul A. Delcourt. 1977. Presettlement Magnolia-Beech Climax of the Gulf Coastal Plain: Quantitative Evidence from the Apalachicola River Bluffs, North-Central Florida. *Ecology* 58:1085–1093.

Dickinson, Joshua C. III. 1969. Eucalyptus in the Sierra of Southern Peru. *Geographical Review* 59:294–307.

Downing, A. J. 1991 (1850). A Treatise on the Theory and Practice of Landscape Gardening Adapted to North America. Dumbarton Oaks Research Library and Collection, Washington, D.C.

Duhe, Brian J. 1980. Utilization of Acorns from the Live Oak (*Quercus virginiana*) as Food by Prehistoric People in Coastal Louisiana. Unpublished manuscript.

Dunbar, Linda Ann. 1991. The Live Oak: Symbol of the South Carolina Lowcountry. Unpublished M.A. thesis, University of North Carolina at Chapel Hill.

Dunn, Mary Eubanks. 1983. Coquille Flora (Louisiana): An Ethnobotanical Reconstruction. *Economic Botany* 37:349–359.

Dysart, Lyn J. 1968. Famous Old Oak Defies Destruction after Death. The Times-Picayune (New Orleans), p. 5.

Elbow, Gary S. 1975. The Plaza and the Park: Factors in the Differentiation of Guatemalan Town Squares. *Growth and Change* 6:14–18.

Eliade, Mircea. 1969. Images and Symbols: Studies in Religious Symbolism. New York: Sheed and Ward.

Elmqvist, T., P. Cox, W. Rainey, and E. Pierson. 1992. Restricted Pollination on Oceanic Islands: Pollination of *Ceiba pentandra* by Flying Foxes in Samoa. Biotropica 24:15–23.

Entrikin, J. Nicholas. 1991. The Betweenness of Place. Baltimore: Johns Hopkins University Press.

Evelyn, John. 1972 (1662). Silva: Or, A Discourse on Forest Trees. York, England: J. Dodsley.

Evernden, Neil. 1992. The Social Creation of Nature. Baltimore and London: Johns Hopkins University Press.

Feltwell, John, and Neil G. Odenwald. 1992. Live Oak Splendor: Gardens along the Mississippi from Natchez to New Orleans. Dallas: Taylor.

Folan, William, Ellen R. Kintz, and Laraine A. Fletcher. 1983. Coba: A Classic Maya Metropolis. New York and London: Academic Press.

Fowells, H. A., comp. 1965. Silvics of Forest Trees of the United States. Washington, D.C.: U.S. Department of Agriculture, Forest Service.

Francaviglia, Richard. 1978. The Mormon Landscape: Existence, Creation, and Perception of an Image in the American West. New York: AMS Press.

Frazer, James George. 1966 (1922). The Golden Bough: A Study in Magic and Religion. London: Macmillan.

Friedrich, Paul. 1970. Proto-Indo-European Trees: The Arboreal System of a Prehistoric People. Chicago and London: University of Chicago Press.

Gade, Daniel W. 1976a. The Latin American Central Plaza as a Functional Space. In: Latin America: Search for Geographic Explanations. Proceedings of the Conference of Latin Americanist Geographers. Vol. 5. Ed. R. J. Tate, 16–23.

———. 1976b. Naturalization of Plant Aliens: The Volunteer Orange in Paraguay. *Journal of Biogeography* 3:269–279.

———. 1999. Nature and Culture in the Andes. Madison: University of Wisconsin Press.

Gadgil, Madhav, and V. D. Vartak. 1976. The Sacred Groves of Western Ghats in India. *Economic Botany* 30:152–160.

Glacken, Clarence J. 1967. Traces on the Rhodian Shore: Nature and Culture in Western Thought from Ancient Times to the End of the Eighteenth Century. Berkeley: University of California Press.

Gonzalez Ayala, Julio Cesar. 1992. La Ceiba. *Pianka* 4:3–4.

Gottlieb, Alma. 1992. Under the Kapok Tree: Identity and Difference in Beng Thought. Bloomington and Indianapolis: Indiana University Press.

Greller, Andrew M. 1990. Comparison of Humid Forest Zones in Eastern Mexico and Southeastern United States. *Bulletin of the Torrey Botanical Club* 117:382–396.

Guest, Gregory S. 1995. A Tree for All Reasons: The Maya and the "Sacred" Ceiba (Yucatan). Unpublished M.A. thesis, University of Calgary, Canada.

Haag, William G. 1971. Louisiana in North American Prehistory. Mélanges no.

1. Baton Rouge: Museum of Geoscience, Louisiana State University.

Haines, Roy. 1973. Friendship Oak Has Role in Coast Tree Replanting. Times-Picayune (New Orleans), January 28, Section 1, p. 3.

Haller, John M. 1985. The Giant Ceiba of Palín. *American Forests:* 48–50, 62–63.

Harlan, Jack R., Jan M. J. De Wet, and Ann B. L. Stemler, eds. 1976. Origins of African Plant Domestication. The Hague: Mouton.

Harlow, William M., and Ellwood S. Harrar. 1958. Textbook of Dendrology. New York: McGraw-Hill.

Heerwagen, Judith, and Gordon Orians. 1994. Humans, Habitats, and Aesthetics. In: The Biophilia Hypothesis. Ed. Stephen Kellert and Edward O. Wilson, 138–172. Washington, D.C.: Island Press.

Hoskins, W. G. 1956. The Making of the English Landscape. London: Hodder and Stoughton, Ltd.

Howe, Marshall Avery. 1906. Some Photographs of the Silk-Cotton Tree (*Ceiba pentandra*), with Remarks on the Early Records of Its Occurrence in America. *Torreya* 6:217–231.

Hudson, Charles. 1976. The Southeastern Indians. Knoxville: University of Tennessee Press.

Hutchinson, J. 1967. The Genera of Flowering Plants. Oxford: Clarendon Press.

Jackson, J. B. 1952a. Editorial. *Landscape* 2:6.

———. 1952b. First Interpreter of American Beauty: A. J. Downing and the Planned Landscape. *Landscape* 1:11–18.

Jones, Michael R., and W. Richard Rossman. 1988. A New Era in Urban Forestry. *Journal of Arboriculture* 14:12–17.

Jung, Carl G. 1958. Psyche and Symbol: A Selection from the Writings of C. G. Jung. Ed. Violet S. de Laszlo. Garden City, N.Y.: Doubleday.

———. 1976. Symbols of Transformation. Translated by R. F. C Hull. Bollingen Series 20. Princeton: Princeton University Press.

Kahn, Peter K., and Stephen Kellert, eds. 2002. Children and Nature: Psychological, Sociocultural and Evolutionary Investigations. Cambridge: MIT Press.

Katz, Cindi, and Andrew Kirby. 1991. In the Nature of Things: The Environment and Everyday Life. *Transactions of the Institute of British Geographers* 16:259–271.

Kellert, Stephen R., and Edward O. Wilson, eds. 1993. The Biophilia Hypothesis. Washington, D.C.: Island Press.

Kniffen, Fred B., and Malcolm L. Comeaux. 1979. The Spanish Moss Folk Industry of Louisiana. Mélanges no. 12. Baton Rouge: Museum of Geoscience, Louisiana State University.

Kniffen, Fred B., Hiram F. Gregory, and George A. Stokes. 1987. The Historic Indian Tribes of Louisiana: From 1542 to the Present. Baton Rouge: Louisiana State University Press.

Lawrence, Henry W. 1988. Origins of the Tree-Lined Boulevard. *Geographical Review* 78:355–374.

———. 1993. The Greening of the Squares of London: Transformation of

Urban Landscapes and Ideals. *Annals of the Association of American Geographers* 83:90–118.

Lawson, John. 1966 (1709). A New Voyage to Carolina. Ann Arbor: University Microfilms, Inc.

Lewington, Anna, and Edward Parker. 1999. Ancient Trees: Trees That Live for a Thousand Years. London: Collins and Brown.

Longfellow, Henry W. 1964. Evangeline. New York: Aventine Press.

Low, Setha M. 1993. Cultural Meaning of the Plaza: The History of the Spanish-American Gridplan-Plaza Urban Design. In: The Cultural Meaning of Urban Space. Ed. Robert Rotenberg and Gary McDonogh, 75–94. Westport, Conn.: Bergin and Garvey.

Lundell, Cyrus. 1937. The Vegetation of Petén. Washington, D.C.: Carnegie Institution of Washington.

Majupuria, Trilok Chandra. 1989. Religious and Useful Plants of Nepal and India. Lalitpur Colony, Lashkar, India: M. Gupta.

Martin, Alexander, Herbert Zim, and Arnold Nelson. 1951. American Wildlife and Plants. New York: Dover.

Maynard, Eileen A. 1963. The Women of Palín: A Comparative Study of Indian and Ladino Women in a Guatemalan Village. Unpublished Ph.D. diss., Department of Anthropology, Cornell University.

McPherson, E. Gregory, and Renee A. Haip. 1989. Emerging Desert Landscape in Tucson. *Geographical Review* 79:435–449.

Meinig, D. W., ed. 1979. The Interpretation of Ordinary Landscapes. New York and Oxford: Oxford University Press.

Merchant, Carolyn. 1992. Radical Ecology: The Search for a Livable World. New York: Routledge.

Meyer, Jeffrey G. 2001. America's Famous and Historic Trees: From George Washington's Tulip Poplar to Elvis Presley's Pin Oak. New York: Houghton Mifflin.

Mikesell, Marvin. 1969. The Deforestation of Mount Lebanon. Geographical Review 59:1–28.

Muir, John. 1981. A Thousand-Mile Walk to the Gulf. Boston: Houghton Mifflin.

Murawski, D., and J. Hamrick. 1992. Mating System and Phenology of *Ceiba Pentandra* (Bombacaceae) in Central Panama. The Journal of Heredity 83:401–404.

Nakagawa, Tadashi. 1987. The Cemetery as a Cultural Manifestation: Louisiana Necrogeography. Unpublished Ph.D. diss., Louisiana State University.

Neal, Marie. 1949. In Gardens of Hawaii. Honolulu: Bernice P. Bishop Museum.

Newton, Milton B., ed. 1985. The Journal of John Landreth, Surveyor. Baton Rouge: Geoscience Publications, Department of Geography and Anthropology, Louisiana State University.

Nicholson, Katharine S. 1922. Historic American Trees. New York: Frye.

Nixon, W. 1984. A Biosystematic Study of *Quercus* series *Virentes* (the Live Oaks) with Phylogenetic Analyses of Fagales, Fagaceae and Quercus. Unpublished Ph.D. diss, University of Texas at Austin.

Nolan, Mary Lee. 1986. Pilgrimage Traditions and the Nature Mystique in Western European Culture. *Journal of Cultural Geography* 7(1):5–20.

Odenwald, Neil, and James Turner. 1987. Identification, Selection and Use of Southern Plants for Landscape Design. Baton Rouge: Claitor's Publishing Division.

Orso, Ethelyn. 1992. Louisiana Live Oak Lore. Lafayette: Center for Louisiana Studies, University of Southwestern Louisiana.

Packenham, Thomas. 1997. Meetings with Remarkable Trees. New York: Random House.

Parsons, James J. 1962. The Acorn-Hog Economy of the Oak Woodlands of Southwestern Spain. *Geographical Review* 52:211–235.

Pennington, Estill Curtis. 1991. Downriver: Currents of Style in Louisiana Painting 1800–1950. Gretna, La.: Pelican.

Pennington, T. Q., and Sarukhan, José. 1960. Árboles Tropicales de México. Mexico City: Instituto Nacional de Investigaciones Forestales.

Platt, William J., and Mark W. Schwartz. 1990. Temperate Hardwood Forests. In Ecosystems of Florida. Ed. J. Ewel Myers, 194–229.

Pliny. 1952. Natural History. London: W. Heinemann. Harvard Classics Library.

Polonsky Celcer, Enrique, ed. 1962. Monografía Antológica del Árbol. Guatemala: Centro Editorial "Jose de Pineda Ibarra."

Post, Lauren C. 1974. Cajun Sketches from the Prairies of Southwestern Louisiana. Baton Rouge: Louisiana State University Press.

Preston, Dickson. 1972. Wye Oak: The History of a Great Tree. Cambridge, Md.: Tidewater.

Price, Larry W. 1993. Hedges and Shelterbelts on the Canterbury Plains, New Zealand: Transformation of an Antipodean Landscape. *Annals of the Association of American Geographers* 83:119–140.

Proyecto Guauhitemala. 1992. Guauhitemala: Lugar des Bosques. Guatemala: Asociación Becaria Guatemalteca.

Rackham, Oliver. 1976. Trees and Woodland in the British Landscape. London: J. M. Dent.

Randall, Charles, and Henry Clapper. 1976. Famous and Historic Trees. Washington D.C.: American Forestry Association.

Rapoport, Amos. 1990. The Meaning of the Built Environment: A Nonverbal Communication Approach. Tucson: University of Arizona Press.

Rashford, John. 1985. The Cotton Tree and the Spiritual Realm in Jamaica. *Jamaica Journal* 18(1):49–57.

Ratzel, Friedrich. 1988. Sketches of Urban and Cultural Life in North America. New Brunswick and London: Rutgers University Press.

Record, Samuel J., and Robert W. Hess. 1943. Timbers of the World. New Haven: Yale University Press.

Redfield, Robert. 1936. The Coati and the Ceiba. Maya Research 3:231–243.

Richans, R. H. 1983. Elm. Cambridge: Cambridge University Press.

Richardson, Miles. 1978. La Plaza como Lugar Social: El Papel del Lugar en el Encuentro Humano. *Vínculos: Revista de Antropología del Museo Nacional, Costa Rica* 4:1–20.

Richardson, Miles. 1989. Place and Culture: Two Disciplines, Two Concepts, Two Images of Christ and a Single Goal. In: The Power of Place. Ed. John A. Agnew and James S. Duncan. Boston: Unwin Hyman.

Richardson, Miles, and Robert Dunton. 1989. Culture in Its Places: A Humanistic Presentation. In: The Relevance of Culture. Ed. Morris Freilich, 75–89. New York: Bering and Garvey.

Rival, Laura, ed. 1998. The Social Life of Trees: Anthropological Perspectives on Tree Symbolism. Oxford and New York: Berg.

Robbins, Jim. 2001. A Tree Project Helps the Genes of Champions Live On. New York Times, July 10.

Rodrigue, George. 1976. The Cajuns of George Rodrigue. Birmingham, Ala.: Oxmoor House.

Rykels, Brenda Barger. 1991. Our River Road heritage: The Politics of Land Use: A Study of the History and Preservation Process at Whitney Plantation, St. John the Baptist Parish, Louisiana. Final project. Louisiana State University, School of Landscape Architecture.

Sahagún, Bernardino de. 1950. General History of the Things of New Spain: Florentine Codex. Trans. Arthur J. O. Anderson and Charles E. Dibble. Santa Fe, N.M.: School of American Research.

Sanchez Vindas, Pablo Enrique. 1983. Florula del Parque Nacional Cahuita. San Jose, Costa Rica: Editorial Universidad Estatal a Distancia.

Sapper, Karl. 1897. Das Nordliche Mittel-Amerika Nebst einem Ausflug nach dem Hochland von Anahuác: Reisen und Studien aus den Jahren 1888–1895. Braunschweig, Germany.

Sauer, Carl O. 1971. Sixteenth-Century North America: The Land and the People as Seen by the Europeans. Berkeley: University of California Press.

Schama, Simon. 1995. Landscape and Memory. New York: A. A. Knopf.

Schele, Linda, and David Freidel. 1990. A Forest of Kings: The Untold Story of the Ancient Maya. New York: Morrow.

Schorger, Arlie. 1973. The Passenger Pigeon: Its Natural History and Extinction. Norman: University of Oklahoma Press.

Seeland, Klaus, ed. 1997. Nature Is Culture: Indigenous Knowledge and Sociocultural Aspects of Trees and Forests in Non-European Cultures. London: Intermediate Technology Publications.

Semple, Ellen Churchill. 1931. The Geography of the Mediterranean Region: Its Relation to Ancient History. New York: Henry Holt.

Sharer, Robert J. 1994. The Ancient Maya. Stanford: Stanford University Press.

Silver, Timothy. 1990. A New Face on the Countryside: Indians, Colonists and Slaves in South Atlantic Forests, 1500–1800. Cambridge: Cambridge University Press.

Simoons, Frederick J. 1998. Plants of Life, Plants of Death. Madison: University of Wisconsin Press.

Smith, J. R. 1916. The Oak Tree and Man's Environment. *Geographical Review* 1:3–19.

Smith, J. Russell. 1987. Tree Crops: A Permanent Agriculture. Washington, D.C.: Island Press.

Soza, José María. 1957. Pequeña Monografía del Departamento de Petén. Guatemala: Editorial del Ministro de Educación Pública.

Spradley, James P. 1980. Participant Observation. New York: Holt, Rinehart and Winston.

Standley, Paul C. 1923. Trees and Shrubs of Mexico. Washington, D.C.: Smithsonian Institution. Contributions from the United States National Herbarium, 23.

Standley, Paul C., and Julian A. Steyermark. 1949. Flora of Guatemala. Chicago: Chicago Natural History Museum. Fieldiana: Botany, 24.

Stephens, Edwin L. 1931. How Old Are the Live Oaks? *American Forests* 37:739–742.

———. 1934. "I Saw in Louisiana a Live Oak Growing." *Louisiana Conservation Review* 4:17–22.

Stielow, Frederick J 1975. Isolation and Development on a Louisiana Gulfcoast Island: Grand Isle, 1781–1962. Unpublished Ph.D. diss., Indiana University.

Stilgoe, John R. 1995. Boyhood Landscape and Repetition. In: Landscape in America. Ed. George Thompson, 183–202. Austin: University of Texas Press.

Stoll, Otto. 1886. Guatemala: Reisen und Schilderungen aus den Jahren 1878–1883. Leipzig: F. A. Brockhaus.

Stone, Christopher D. 1974. Should Trees Have Standing? Toward Legal Rights for Natural Objects. Los Altos, Calif.: William Kaufmann.

Sutton, Richard K. 1982. The Image of a Garden: Vernacular Conifer Plantings in the Rural Landscape of Otoe County, Nebraska. *Pioneer America* 14:93–114.

Swanton, J. R. 1911. Indian Tribes of the Lower Mississippi Valley and Adjacent Coast of the Gulf of Mexico. Washington, D.C.: U.S. Government Printing Office. Bureau of American Ethnology, Bulletin 43.

Thompson, Phil. 1995. Campus Live Oak Survey and Stress Analysis. Office of Facility Development, Louisiana State University.

Toledo, Victor Manuel. 1976. Pollination of Some Rain Forest Plants by Non-Hovering Birds in Veracruz, Mexico. *Biotropica* 8:262–267.

Tolkien, J. R. R. 1973. The Two Towers. New York: Houghton Mifflin.

Tompkins, Janet. 1994. Romancing the Oak. *Forests and People* 44(3):4–7.

Tuan, Yi-Fu. 1991. Language and the Making of Place: A Narrative-Descriptive Approach. *Annals of the Association of American Geographers* 81:684–696.

———. 1993. Passing Strange and Wonderful: Aesthetics, Nature, and Culture. Washington, D.C.: Island Press.

Turnbull, Martha. 1855–1894. Unpublished Diaries. Turnbull-Bowman-Lyons

Family Papers, 1797–1955. Hill Memorial Library, Louisiana and Lower Mississippi Valley Collection, Louisiana State University.

Ulrich, R. S. 1984. View through a Window May Influence Recovery from Surgery. *Science* 224:420–421.

Vale, Thomas. 1982. Plants and People. Washington, D.C.: Association of American Geographers. Resource Publications in Geography.

Van Doren, Mark, ed. 1928. Travels of William Bartram. Dover, N.H.: Dover Publications.

Vega, Luis Rosado. 1938. Amerindmaya. Mexico City: Ediciones Botas.

Villagutierre Soto-Mayor, Don Juan de. 1983. History of the Conquest of the Province of the Itza: Subjugation and Events of the Lacandon and Other Nations of Uncivilized Indians in the Lands from the Kingdom of Guatemala to the Provinces of Yucatan in North America. Lancaster, Calif.: Labyrinthos.

von Maltzahn, Kraft E. 1994. Nature as Landscape: Dwelling and Understanding. Montreal and Kingston: McGill-Queen's University Press.

Voorhies, Felix. 1977 (1907). Acadian Reminiscences: The True Story of Evangeline. Lafayette, University of Southwestern Louisiana.

Waugh, Frank A., ed. 1921. Downing's Landscape Gardening. New York: Wiley.

Weekes, William D. 1979. The Awesome Live Oak. *American Forests* 85:20–23, 56–59.

Whitman, Walt. 1931. Leaves of Grass. New York: Aventine Press.

Winberry, John. 1979. The Osage Orange, a Botanical Artifact. *Pioneer America: The Journal of Historic American Material Culture* 11:134–141.

Wood, Virginia Steele. 1981. Live Oaking: Southern Timber for Tall Ships. Boston: Northeastern University Press.

Writers' Program, Works Projects Administration. 1941. Louisiana: A Guide to the State. New York: Hastings House. American Guide Series.

Zand, Stephen J. 1941. Kapok: A Survey of Its History, Cultivation and Uses with Special Consideration of Its Application to Thermal and Acoustic Treatments. New York: Lincoln Engraving and Printing Corp.

Zube, Ervin H. 1978. The Natural History of Urban Trees. In: Humanscape: Environments for People. Ed. Stephen Kaplan and Rachel Kaplan, 178–187. North Scituate, Mass.: Duxbury Press.

INDEX

Lightning Source UK Ltd.
Milton Keynes UK
UKHW020326231222
414339UK00012BA/1223